AHA!

The Realization Book

Vywamus
through Janet McClure and Lillian Harben

Light
Technology
Publishing

Books by Vywamus
through Janet McClure

Light Techniques That Trigger Transformation

The Source Adventure

Scopes of Dimensions:
How to Experience Multi-Dimensional Reality

Channeling: The Natural State [German]

AHA! The Realization Book

The Story of Sanat Kumara: Training a Planetary Logos

Evolution: Our Loop of Experiencing

✧　✧　✧

Copyright 1990 by The Tibetan Foundation

First Printing 1990
ISBN 0-929385-14-4

Second Printing 1995
ISBN 0-929385-61-6

Published by

Printed by

**MISSION
POSSIBLE**
Commercial
Printing

Light Technology Publishing
P.O. Box 1526
Sedona, AZ 86339

P.O. Box 1495
Sedona, AZ 86339

Introduction to Vywamus

Vywamus is a great being, a cosmic being who has come among us to serve during these critical, yet marvelous times when humanity seeks to evolve into spiritual consciousness, casting off the outworn "forms" and moving into a greater light, into the New Age. He tells us that he was invoked by humanity's desire to evolve and came here, as many spiritual teachers are now doing, to make this transition as painless and smooth as possible, and at as high a vibrational level as possible.

Vywamus is a higher aspect of Sanat Kumara, our Planetary Logos who ensouls the Earth and all upon and within it. The Earth, in effect, is being held together by his consciousness. Vywamus can be equated to the soul of Sanat Kumara.

Long ago Vywamus chose to express in physical existence and evolved through the physical chain just as humanity on this planet has chosen to do. He evolved on a planet far distant from here but one that was similar to the Earth. While in physical existence he was offered the opportunity to be a channel for a very high spiritual teacher. He feels that by thus serving he was able to gain clear perception of the nature of existence and evolving consciousness which enabled him to ascend in his next life. Ascension was accomplished after only 37 incarnations in the physical. Because of the experience of his rapid gain in evolution due to his channeling, he encourages his students to learn to channel, not only as a service to bring the spiritual teacher's message to Earth, but to aid their own development.

Now in his great love Vywamus has chosen to aid mankind

through dedicated channels such as Janet McClure, and he offers his teachings through classes and personal work as well as through sound, which is one of his specialties.

Introduction

What is a realization? It is the bringing together, making real, understanding of where you are now with respect to a certain area of your life, usually a certain large area in your life. It is where you are and how you arrived there. Suddenly something that you didn't see or understand previously becomes crystal clear, especially to the mental body.

If you recognize that you create your own life from your beliefs about yourself (and this book is based upon that premise), then you know also that you can change your life, improve it by changing the beliefs that are not serving you well.

When you see an effect, a situation that you are mirroring, it is possible to work backward or deduce what belief you are holding that causes this effect that you have created in your life. At least you can look at various possibilities that might be producing this effect. For instance, if you do not have enough money, if there is a lack of abundance in your life, then it stands to reason that your beliefs must be that: (1) You are not creative enough to produce abundance, (2) You don't deserve abundance, (3) Having abundance is not spiritual and you must choose between living a good life or having abundance, and (4) It is dangerous to your physical existence to have abundance.

Now this programming is not apparent to your conscious mind because it is subconscious, so of course you will say to yourself, "Certainly I believe that I deserve abundance." But know that if you were not holding a contrary belief you would have it, as it is your birthright. Once you see the picture of why you brought this particular situation into your life and why you are holding it, once you see the whole picture in the present time and not as a pattern that is being played over and over by your subconscious, then you can disconnect from the old pattern. Now sometimes you don't even have to do this consciously, as the mechanisms will do it automatically for you.

Usually, however, to make a complete change it is necessary to recognize or realize more than just mentally. YOUR EMOTIONAL BODY'S BELIEFS AND NEEDS MUST BE MET. The emotional body needs to feel supported as you change this pattern. The emotional works through feelings and symbols, but its conclusions are just as valid, just as meaningful and even more powerful than the mental conclusions. The mental often needs to convince the emotional of its conclusion concerning the erroneous belief that the subconscious is holding. The emotional body is operating from this belief and so it must be convinced that it will be supported in this new belief or pattern that you are trying to set up.

For instance, perhaps you have drowned in several lifetimes. The fear comes up again as you approach water in this life, for there is a carry-over of this information, this emotionally charged pattern, from one life to the next. If that emotional body can now feel supported and feel that the water will support your body, then it will not fear that it will be in danger again. If it goes into agreement with your mental realization and releases the fear as the mental is releasing the perception, then you can swim without fear and let the water support you.

In this book, I, Vywamus have given many possible causes of a lot of undesirable or unclear circumstances that you may be mirroring in your life. You can read the chapters and see if they seem to apply to what you are mirroring into your life from your beliefs.

If you are manifesting into your life in a way that is not clear, then reading this book may give you a "light bulb" or a realization that you are holding a specific erroneous belief.

I hope that you will read through the whole book even if you are looking for a particular situation, because I believe some of these chapters will surprise you in their view of what I see from my view. Perhaps that will point to areas you can change to bring in some special opportunities that you have never activated before.

Love, Vywamus

Lillian Harben

Lillian Harben was vice president and chief executive officer of The Tibetan Foundation, Inc., a spiritual vehicle for the Hierarchy of the Planet. She was raised in Detroit, received her B.S.M.E. degree there, and worked there in various engineering facilities doing computer analysis.

Lillian was interested in and studied metaphysics with several teachers, including Dr. Doreal of The Brotherhood of the White Temple. For many years she channeled Thoth, the teacher honored in Egyptian mythology as the God of Art and Science. She has been associated with Thoth through many lifetimes. She now channels Vywamus and occasionally other teachers.

In 1983, when The Tibetan Foundation was launched, Lillian was part of a small group working with Janet, and she continued to be active in its development as a vehicle of transformation to aid humanity and the Earth in the New Age. She is known especially for her realization work in the Foundation. The Foundation was disbanded after Janet died, and Lillian now gives workshops, readings and intensives out of her home. She can be reached at:

(602) 974-5217.

Janet McClure

Janet studied intensively for many years with a spiritual teacher and received her Doctor of Metaphysics degree from The Brotherhood of the White Temple. She had already dedicated her life to the service of the Cosmic Plan when she was asked by Djwhal Khul to assist him in aiding humanity by being a conscious channel for his energies and spiritual teachings. Djwhal was responding to a request from Sanat Kumara, the Planetary Logos who ensouls the Earth, to return to his Earth contacts and once again aid humanity as he had done forty years earlier through Alice Bailey and her books.

Djwhal knew that channeling would flow easily for Janet, as she had had extensive channeling experience in previous lives and had taught channeling in ancient Egypt. Janet enthusiastically put aside her familiar and comfortable world of business and committed herself to this new mission. Being an Aries, Janet's nature was to move forward with her New Age awareness, secure in the knowledge of the support she would receive from the Source.

After channeling Djwhal for two years, Janet was introduced by him to the cosmic being Vywamus, a caring and loving being who is a light aspect of Sanat Kumara. Vywamus was attracted to the beautiful light of the Earth and continued the work with Janet that Djwhal began in 1982.

The teachers were very interested in bringing their information to Earth through a group focus. Because Janet was already working with a dedicated group, and this group's energies were compatible with the teachers, the entire group was asked to work together and form The Tibetan Foundation. The group had been learning specific methods to remove and clear the blocks in the subconscious belief structure. These blocks come from our false beliefs that have accumulated through all our past lives and can create resistance in our present life to moving forward with our development. These methods were practiced and patterned into the techniques used today by The Tibetan Foundation. Workshops, classes and personal appointments were made available to identify the source of the false belief and to guide the participants with affirmations and pattern-removal procedures to clear their blocks and replace them with positive supportive truths.

The Tibetan Foundation was incorporated in January 1983 with Janet as its president. The purpose of the Foundation was to spread the teachings of the spiritual masters to all of humanity. Through lectures, seminars, workshops, correspondence courses, personal appointments, books and transcripts, The Tibetan Foundation achieved its purpose in the United States, Canada and Europe. The information channeled through Janet and the other certified channels brought transformation both to the channels and to thousands who participated in the Foundation events.

Vywamus encourages the training of channels, as he believes channeling to be the single most important step we can take to move forward in our evolution. Concerning her own evolution, Janet said, "The benefits I have received by channeling in terms of clearing blocked areas for myself are enormous. My evolution has accelerated greatly through the channeling process." She left her body in Egypt in Autumn 1990.

Contents

1

Lightening Your Perspective

This chapter talks about light, and certainly you recognize that you are light in manifestation. But you may not recognize that this light perspective is an actual spectrum of energy which varies in its vibrational intensity and which is ever moving, ever changing, ever accelerating, ever evolving. You may have thought of light as simply light without recognizing its growth factor.

Light contains everything that the Source has chosen to manifest within a particular conceptual framework. This Cosmic Day's theme is "courage," thus the light that is manifesting and which we are a part of is an overall, unlimited, evolving, growing perspective focused through the area of courage. This means that you view light through a tone or a focus of courage, and perhaps your beliefs in the area of courage are always affecting your perspective of how you view light, both within yourself and within the divine environment. Can you see that our Source has placed an unlimited and yet evolving perspective which lights up the courage area and allows it to be explored in as complete a manner as the Source's parts or aspects (which are all of us, of course!) can allow. This growing allowingness amplifies and radiates through courage.

Courage as the theme of the day, be it a Cosmic Day or a physical day in which you are involved, is a very special quality which makes all things possible. You are courageous when you allow, through your divine connection, a growing perspective to be present, a "lightening" perspective in any area of your life. You may have fears in allowing your unlimitedness to be expressed. Some of you fear standing in front of large groups. If those fears are present and your commitment level makes it necessary to address a large group, then the area of courage used through this commitment level can make possible what you yet fear. It can help you move through the fears into a more unlimited expression. You may ask, "What is the difference between courage and commitment?" Indeed it is a valid question. Commitment, in my opinion, is the basic cornerstone, the basic heart quality which make everything else possible. It is the connector into the Plan, it is the link through which everything else flows. It seems to me that courage in this case could be the energy flowing through the commitment area, allowing the beginning of a clearer and more unlimited perspective.

Courage, then, is energy and when you put energy into something it will make a difference, it will help you to become more unlimited. At first it may be necessary to clean out any particular subconscious blocks, but the lightening process, using the energy of courage, will allow you to make contact gradually, one step at a time, with your more unlimited perspective. It is no accident that courage is the specific quality needed at this time by all of you to create the New Age. The courage is needed to stand up for your convictions or beliefs at particular times when not doing so would allow old patterns of behavior to control you. Having the courage of your convictions through your commitment to serve the Cosmic Plan opens then new opportunities and a perspective of how to be ever lighter, ever aware of light as the movement, as the flow, as the organizer in existence.

Moving on to that perspective of light as an organizer, you can see that that is true by looking at a rainbow. The light is broken down into specific colors which, when radiated together, create the whole spectrum of light. On the physical plane you don't see too much of the light spectrum, but it certainly is growing, meaning that you are all seeing the higher or more radiant colors. Since the Harmonic Convergence the deeper blues, reds, violets and yes, oranges – the very deep gold, these radiant, electrical colors from this more "excitable" part of the light spectrum are being seen, are being felt, are beginning to be utilized. You may ask, what do I mean about "excitable?" Well, I certainly do not mean it in a negative sense, but you have ever gotten excited about a new project and that excitement gave you the enthusiasm and the desire to create and you accomplished much in this area? Thus creative "excitability" is a part of the movement or progressive awareness which has been termed the New Age.

The light perspective is literally interwoven. Although a rainbow is nice and neat in its differentiation of the colors, a clearer perspective is to see all colors as having the capacity to interact with every other color oranges and reds and blues and yellows and greens and violets, even the pinks, silvers and golds, each color having full capacity to interact or be a part of every other color. Thus, if one particular color is not yet able to interact totally through you, this is a block which creates an inability to see yourself completely as an integrated light perspective. Let me give you an example. The color red is associated with the dynamic energy. If you have blocks in the area of the dynamic energy, your light perspective may not yet be integrating red, so that your red aspect, if you will, may be "dragging its feet" as far as allowing yourself to be fully integrated light. Now, the goal is to use your body of light as your vehicle on the Earth, but again one must clear each color and its symbolic association/references so that full integration can take place. I give you below a brief color list and its association. Although this information may be available in many places, I want you to be able to refer to it in this material, in this chapter on light, so that you may seek right here and now as you read this to see which aspects you need to be clearer on. You may wish to take an Intensive with the Foundation to dig around, if you will, in the subconscious mind if you find certain colors not responding in an integrated manner. Let us then give you each color and its correspondence and some exercises to use in finding out how you are doing in blending your body of light or lightening your perspective.

Our rainbow will be rather creative, not necessarily the traditional rainbow at all.

Red: The dynamic energy associated many times with thrusting into new/unknown areas. Your association with the male polarity, whether you are in a male or female body, your association with the evolutionary process and, for many of you, with the evolving Source.

Orange: The mental body, in both its logical and conceptual form, your association with structure or organization. Your ability to see the whole picture in any situation and in your life and in regard to the whole. Your ability to use the fifth dimension. For many of you this color links you into a crystalline association with the mineral kingdom on the Earth. For about 50% of you there is a link here into the overall energy grid system associated with the Earth.

Yellow: This color is associated with clear thinking, intelligence and the means to free misperceptions through a magnification process. Has third-dimension transformational qualities. It has healing associations, especially when the healing moves through the Earth and back into the individual. Helps focus or gather energy together, thus helps the mental qualities to be more focused, addresses scattering and the memory area, connects directly with the physical aspects of Sanat Kumara and thus forms a chain or linkage to the Solar Logos, Helios. In this connection also see the color gold.

Green: Associated with healing, associated with growth and evolution, associated with harmony and tranquillity. Associated with a clear use of the emotional body, specific connection to the fourth dimension, has an artistic development connection, including painting, music and dance. Is able to draw from the Source level itself a perspective of wholeness, thus addresses the area of allowing unlimitedness.

Blue: Blue helps balance the polarity area through the association of love and wisdom. It is an opener and a carrier of the electrical or silver energy they blend together as the body becomes lighter. Is associated with purity of purpose and love. Helps to clarify the purpose area through balancing and blending. Emphasis on service to the Plan, keeps lighting up the Plan.

Indigo: Identifies a deep Source-level connection and holds a focus on it. Helps to clear areas concerning separation. Has often been associated with the Christ Consciousness energy, seeks to blend spiritual perspectives through a decrystallizing process. Decrystallizes in the surrender area, has seven levels which decrystallize as one "ascends" through them.

Violet: Transformation. Purification, transmutation, what has been called ceremonial "magic" or invoking through an integration of all of the other colors and what they represent. Helps integrate all of what has been learned on Earth, helps heal "polarity splits," helps heal the emotional body through its association with the spiritual body, helps cleanse and purify the physical structure, helps align the mental and spiritual perspectives. Closely associated with St. Germaine, closely associated with the New Age.

Pink: Associated with the heart energy and its characteristics, particularly love, compassion and gratitude. Helpful in softening any crystallization in the will area, helps the surrender process and reaches into and supports what is new, what has begun. Thus helpful in realizing divine support. Many times associated with the angelic kingdom.

Silver: It is a symbol for the electrical energy of the soul. Symbolizes the use of the soul's energy, works with being in the flow, will seek to break up or decrystallize blocks in the use of electricity in all its forms, including all electrical and electronic devices used on the Earth. Many times associated with the angelic kingdom. Addresses the lightening perspective, helps deal with blocks in the electrical flow of the physical structure through a penetrative process, helps anchor more of the soul's energy in the cellular level.

Gold: The "perfect integrator." The accepting of the soul level is emphasized. The accepting of wholeness on every level is emphasized. Emphasizes linkage systems. Deals with full abundance. Helps to integrate the cocreator levels, deals with putting together pieces of any area that has seemed scattered. Connects through the Sanat Kumara or the planetary link directly to Helios or the Solar Logos consciousness level. Helps to develop through decrystallization more heart radiance. Seeks to help soften perspectives which need blending and thus they blend more easily. Deals with "kingship/queenship." Deals with assuming one's full power through the true identity level. Awakens within one the true reality level. Broadens the creative base through allowing it to flow. Accelerates blending levels of creativity together. Often acts as a "launching" into an integrated level of creativity.

An exercise to work with the above could be to see each color as a person, personify it as a person wearing that color, or their skin may even be that color, and see what sort of a personification you get. For example: if you are a woman and you personify blue and see it as a woman who is sobbing, feeling lost, dejected, it may be that in the polarity area the female part of you is feeling lonely, not feeling unified or joined with the male part. This is just an example, but by personifying each color, not only will you see what needs to be understood about that color, but by having two colors interact or relate to one another you can learn from that also. Gold might be the color that invites all the others over for a party. Does everyone accept the invitation? Will everyone come? How are they dressed for the party? If it is a formal affair and blue comes in something that is not integratable into the setting gold has created, then look to see what isn't integrating well within the blue perspective. Using these techniques with another person, a partner, and being creative about the settings and the usage of the images can be helpful to you in understanding yourself as light.

Remember, your light perspective which is "lightening" all of the time can be addressed through symbols. There are many ways to use symbols, and instead of a personification you may wish to ask each color to give you a symbol. Place it in the third eye area and then see on a screen what is projected through that symbol. You may also wish to wear the color both within and outside and see what comes up for you as you do. You may wish to put it on the physical body, put it on the emotional body, put it on the mental body and put it on the spiritual body, seeing what sort of a response each body makes in regard to that particular color.

2

Anxiety Patterning

M any of you have a great deal of anxiety and don't know that it is there. There may be a sense of restlessness, difficulty in sleeping, difficulty in concentrating, difficulty in creating a focus that lasts without a wandering effect coming in through this anxiety patterning. Anxiety is created by the mental body in its search for connections.

Now, the mental body often seeks to guide the life rather completely at certain stages in one's evolution. There may not yet be much communication with the emotional body, which is the flow connector. The mental body is a deep probe and conceptual tool but not a connector in the same way that the emotional body is. However, if you are only validating your mental body in your life, it seeks to connect but cannot, so it wanders or considers every alternative, seeking to come full circle and make a point of realization.

Now, you may very well make a mental point of realization. You integrate a certain perspective within you mentally. Let us say that you are seeking to allow yourself to channel more deeply. Mentally you know that you are not going as deep as you would like, and perhaps you've seen certain patterns of behavior that are getting in the way. You have resolved or integrated your understanding into what is desired here, but it is still not connecting for you.

Your mental body, then, trying to do its job, (that is its job, remember) will probe deeper and deeper or perhaps wider and wider. There may be disturbing dreams initiated by your mental body. There may be twitching or tensions, and there certainly is the anxiety patterning as the mental body tries to bridge the gap in the connection to the desired area. Your mental body is not meant to do all things or to be that complete perspective of self. It holds the focus and helps you to develop an overall understanding, but the connection between the two is the emotional body, the desire, the love, the allowingness, the sense of being receptive, the joy. Literally all of these positive emotions are what connects one focus of self to the larger perspective. Certainly they also hopefully connect you into that spiritual perspective, the divine blueprint of self so you can see how your particular divine blueprint fits into the overall divine blueprint.

One of the deepest patterns of anxiety comes in your evolution just before you awaken to a sense that there is something beyond the physical. It happens when you are the most mental, when you are focused most completely and intensely on the mental level, perhaps even ignoring the physical body. This intense concentration has a tendency to alienate, and that alienation, my friends, is anxiety. Whenever there is anxiety there is an alienated or separated perspective that, although it is probing and considering many things, has not found the connection because it is not able to. The emotional body has the clear connecting ability.

Now, you may wish to argue with me a little bit about the mental body's capability. Believe me, my friends, I am not criticizing the mental body. I, Vywamus, have been there, though, as far as being alienated within the mental perspective. Believe me, this was one of the deepest areas which I found important to resolve within myself. I was able, however, through a very good connection with my physical perspective, not yet my emotional, not at that time, to resolve it. And many of you are doing that also. I find it extremely helpful that there is such an emphasis on physical fitness on the Earth now. This is your Earth seeking to break through out of a rather mental vise that is active in some of your civilization.

As we look at the United States and its evolution, we see in the past 50 years a validation of the mental body's strengths without seeing an equal partnership with the emotional, physical and spiritual bodies' perspectives. Your mental body must learn to be a team player. Interestingly enough, the emotional body and its beliefs about your mental perspective are equally a part of the anxiety patterning. I do not, however, find anxiety a part of the emotional perspective. There may be those that disagree with me here. I think anxiety could be called a mental emotion.

Now, I've told some of you that are very mental that you have mental emotions, meaning that the mental body is so much a leader that the only type of emotional response that you have is through the mental body. This is what I am calling a mental emotion then anxiety. It only comes through the mental body's perspective, and what comes through in anxiety patterning is a sense that a connection has not been made in a specific area, or, if the pattern goes deep enough, there may be an overall anxiety about your connection to the Creator.

In your mental institutions, those that move up and down, back and forth, in an agitated manner, those who twitch a lot, those that create a discourse, talk to themselves excitedly, are certainly out of it emotionally also, but the deepest part of their patterning is through the mental body. They are experiencing a pattern of alienation through the mental perspective. To deal with this it is absolutely essential that the emotions begin to be perceived as equal to the mental. That is asking a lot of someone who has buried the emotions lifetime after lifetime. The emotions do not seem to be a team member. They do not seem to be capable of the clear expression that the mental body is capable of. The clear way to get to the emotions, of course, is through the heart center. Your mental body will validate the heart and its positive qualities as important. It may not see them as a part of the emotional body, though. There is within the mental perspective, for some of you, a belief that the negative emotions are all that exist in the emotional body. The heart center is something different. Of course it is not negative. The heart uses the emotional body as its vehicle. But it (the heart) and all of its qualities are fingers that connect all of the bodies. You need each of these fingers or connecting points in order to have the integrated four-body system that you are seeking; they are the connections that you look for as you respond to life mentally.

It is necessary for your mental body to let go of the need to understand everything mentally, because, my friends, some things are not understood mentally, they are understood emotionally, some of them physically and some of them spiritually. Some of the deepest patterning I've seen is in the metaphysical community and says, "I must learn, I must understand it all now." There is such an intensification or an addictive patterning to learning that it wipes out the ability to learn except through the mental responses, and that fractures the learning process and doesn't allow it to be an integrated one.

Many times, for many of you, it impacts the physical body very severely. There are those who have pulled in what could be a death of that physical structure through not being willing to let go and learn through the physical, emotional and spiritual bodies. The mental body must validate evolution on the physical level in order to allow release of anxiety.

You get into anxiety patterns when you can't see a physical effect that is evolving. Now, the heart qualities are the key here, because sometimes it takes more than one lifetime to validate evolution in a particular area. Let me cite as an example the aging process. It may take you many lifetimes to slow down the aging process, and then stop it, and then reverse it, so you cannot always see clearly on the physical level the process that we call evolution. But certainly through your mental body you can see that there is a process, and through your emotional body you can begin to trust the process, and through your spiritual body you make contact with the process. Thus there is the need for your mental body to let go and allow the process to function as completely as possible on the physical level as far as seeing an effect is concerned. The mental body will, of course, continue to process as part of the team.

It is necessary to realize that the process is a fourfold one. Your mental perspective is not asked to understand the emotional perspective, but it is asked to trust the overall perspective that is guiding the system. Now, what does that mean? Didn't I just say that the qualities of the heart are emotional? In one way they are, but trust is a connector. When your mental body sees through a contact with the spiritual that there is an overall Plan and recognizes that it is just one aspect of that Plan, then it releases to allow the other aspects of the Plan to be validated equally through you. That is what I am calling trust.

For most of you the most important point in your evolution on the physical level comes when you raise your head above physicality and take a look and see that there is a spiritual connection. We call this a connection with the soul or a soul-merge. Your mental body recognized something greater and begins what I would call the surrender process to that something greater.

Now, you can't prove the spiritual level to the mental body, and that is one reason why, I, Vywamus, am not willing to manifest miracles for humanity. If you do not recognize mentally yet that there is something greater than that mental perspective or if you do not yet see that the physical level is incomplete without something greater, no one can prove it to you. There may be at a certain point something a teacher can do to show you through your mental body that there is something greater, but, generalizing now, each person must allow that greater level of awareness that is expanding through the strengths of the mental body to be a release or a letting-go process. This is why all compulsions to learn must be released.

If you are reading this and you feel that you must read

everything new, that you must search widely and compulsively to find all that is new, consider the fact that you may even be retarding your evolution by forcing your mental body to be everywhere at once. Now, certainly your mental body with its conceptual abilities can see the whole picture as you allow it to more and more; however, in the process of being on the Earth there is a system, and to find your unique positioning within that system your mental body needs to get out of the way to allow your spiritual body to activate and connect with all of your aspects. When your spiritual perspective is allowed to flood you mentally, emotionally and physically, then the natural connector of the emotional body, your emotional responses, can make that overall connection that you are seeking. Many of you don't know what unconditional love is. Mentally you can't appreciate it, physically you have never felt it, emotionally you are looking for it, but spiritually you already know it, so the spiritual is invoked through the mental's ability to conceive that there is something greater. It brings in a relaxation which takes away the anxiety patterning or the alienated patterning and allows the spiritual to reach that emotional point of view that can then begin the process of connecting you on the physical plane.

Now, we have talked a great deal about the emotional body as being the most resistive. For many of you this is true, but for mainstream humanity it often is the mental perspective that holds a rather rigid perspective of alienation which I am calling anxiety patterning. Now actually the anxiety patterning when full blown is, my friends, a step forward. Isn't that interesting? It says that your mental body is looking for a way to connect. It says the soul is already beginning to influence it.

When there is enough of a surrender mentally, enough of a letting-go, then the anxiety pattern will get better, and the emotional body will be allowed through the mental release to make the beginning or the tentative connections it is seeking.

At that point, then, it is extremely important to look at all of the emotional programming. But particularly you who are very mental must surrender the need to learn, meaning that you are willing to let go of a rigid pattern of learning, knowing that what you are surrendering into is a much larger learning system. But the reason that you haven't let go is because you felt that you had to do it all yourself on the physical level. I tell you to allow yourself to release the need to learn, at least that part of the learning that is compulsive. Certainly I am not telling you to quit learning. That is not my goal, but I am telling you that literally on the physical level there must be a release of a hard line held mentally. You must soften your mental perspective, and releasing that rigidity about learning is the beginning of the more integrated state that you are seeking.

There is always a deep Source-level anxiety, one that looks at the Source relationship and doesn't see the step-by-step process needed to allow the clear level of being that I call the cocreator level to be realized. There is always a Source-level anxiety pattern that says, "Since I can see this concept I should be able to use it mentally right now. The Plan expects me to understand mentally the whole concept, and I should be able to probe into every area now."

I've got news for you, my friend, every area is none of your business now. You are a cocreator. Others have responsibility for certain areas. You have responsibility only for your own area at this point. Certainly cooperation with others is important but you don't have to mentally probe and understand what another already understands. Simply communicate with them and learn from them. But the deep anxiety patterning says, "I must do all this through my mental perspective; that is why the Source has given me a mental body. He expects that of me."

Certainly the Source gave you a mental body and wants you to become unlimited in the use of it, but you are all leaving out the cocreator level when you expect to learn it all now through your own mental body. You have strengths and abilities mentally but you need not encompass all that is in your understanding now. I don't want you to misunderstand me here. Some of you will say to me, "I don't care if I learn it from someone as long as I learn it." But that, for some of you, is a pattern getting into the worthiness area that says, "I am supposed to do it myself but if I can't do it myself then I will allow another to bring it to me but I'll know that I have failed just a little. I'll know that I am alienated a little. I'm not connected deeply enough so I will redouble my effort to learn myself."

Can you see that this becomes a self-defeating pattern? What it is necessary to do eventually is to let go and allow the whole system to be there supporting you — not only your mental perspectives but your spiritual, emotional and physical also. Look deeply into the failure area if you have a lot of anxiety and are trying to allow a more integrated perspective. Look at failure in the sense of being incomplete, of not having enough data.

Mentally things are stored differently than emotionally. When I suggest that you look at an area I mean that you should look at the programming in that area mentally and try to release it.

There may need to be some affirmations, in fact there probably will be. Then look at what sort of an effect you have woven into your life by your anxiety patterning. Have you so impacted the emotional body that it has its own correspondence of the anxiety patterning that functions along with the mental patterning? This is very common, and it is usually the area of support that is affected emotionally. In the area of support (actually nonsupport), you feel you do not have, you are not able to fulfill your responsibilities because of not being allowed to be connected. This emotional correspondence of anxiety shows up, especially in the solar plexus area, and sometimes comes into the physical body so much that you pull in physical illness such as ulcers, colitis, diverticulosis or an intestinal or stomach illness. Those symptoms tell you that the emotional body is definitely affected.

For further discussion of the emotional patterning area I refer you to the following chapters: 3. "Achievement," 4. "Bridging," 5. "Feeling Buried or Overwhelmed," 17. "The Support of Humanity," 18. "Unworthiness and Insecurity," 25. "Accepting One's Divine Power."

3

Achievement

Achievement is a sense of completion, a point of contact with a goal. One seeks to achieve because of a desire to recognize within self the same qualities that one recognizes within the Creator.

The need to achieve, then, is built into the process of evolution. Now, certainly there are several levels of recognition in regard to achievement. The more conscious one is of the whole process of evolution, the more one can see that achievement is literally the evolutionary process that is going on all the time.

One does not feel complete until a specific desired goal has been reached. In an example of running a race the goal is to complete the race. Many see the goal as being first in the race, but the goal is really to run the race, enjoy it, experience it and express the Source as a race runner.

A great sense of achievement comes from helping others, and the reason for that is that it brings into true perspective the way you are meant to live as a cocreator. Of course, helping others needs to be reciprocated, or one needs to accept help from others also, in order for the achievement syndrome to be balanced.

The reason why there are those who are never satisfied with what they achieve is that they don't allow a return flow from that achievement. In order to be happy from helping others the heart must welcome the gratitude, the love, the appreciation of others who have been helped. This, of course, is the return flow that one gets from helping others. It is truly much more comprehensive than it sounds, because when your heart is open enough to receive gratitude and thankfulness, unconditional love and appreciation come into it. This is the means to access a clearer, more magnetic and radiant life perspective.

Thus the achievement from aiding others is a clearer perspective on life, a more comprehensive understanding of self and others and how they fit together. You are not meant to be a martyr or a victim within the process of aiding others. You truly achieve your own greatness through unconditional service. Your own needs are not negated or taken from you or neglected through such service. You choose a different way of referring to your needs, wants and desires. They become caught up in a larger perspective of achievement instead of a point of view that seeks to achieve only from the personal, or what you might call the ego/personality.

The soul has begun to guide the physical life. The desire to achieve becomes a part of the soul's perspective, and the soul in its wider-scoped abilities to see the whole picture puts into divine perspective what is important to achieve and why it is important to release.

At the soul level achievement is as much a release as it is an acquiring. Achievement becomes the balancing perspective from which to view life, and there is great satisfaction in it.

Now, there is a difference between beingness and doingness. In your divine beingness there is absolute perfection and it is beyond achievement, beyond doingness. But this divine perfection is learning and growing and realizing its awakening and expanding joy, love and appreciation and all of the other heart qualities, so it begins to trust so completely that it moves itself into a state of doingness. Trust is the connector here to the Source, which has only the basic desire to express through all of Its parts Its divine state, which is basically a state of appreciation, love, joy, gratitude, etc.

Joy certainly motivates at the highest level, and when one achieves a joyful state, there is such a sense of appreciation, trust, love and supreme confidence in the process of being that an expansion is automatically a part of the process.

In your everyday life, then, what you are seeking to achieve is a happy, fulfilling, successful and balanced life, one in which you will enjoy what you want to do, do what you enjoy and reap an abundant flow as you relate to others in a positive, communicative manner and this allows full expression of who you are.

Some of you, of course, have more specific immediate goals you would like to achieve, but generally what I hear from you are questions about purposes, questions about abundance, questions about happy relationships, questions about how to serve with others. These are motivators, the desire to achieve specific qualities within life. The qualities of life are the qualities of the heart. Once the heart is opened sufficiently life is viewed through these qualities always, and any areas which need resolution or seem blocked can be released; thus achievement in releasing comes through the use of the heart qualities.

You are naturally happy, you are naturally full of trust, you are naturally full of joy and unconditional love. You simply have to achieve a release of those areas which have become a little blocked in order to express these divine qualities.

Achievement, then, is not only moving toward a specific goal but it is a releasing mechanism or motivation that clears out the heart area. I do refer you to the chapter on the qualities of the heart. Read about them and understand as much as you can through the studying process about these qualities. Each time you experientially expand your heart energy, you allow yourself to achieve a clearer life. Certainly you all had moments when you were very grateful to another, when you were full of unconditional love. To remain always in that space, to achieve complete balance and a sense of purposefully being a part of something larger is your goal. You wish to develop that grateful state that acknowledges the Plan as the motivator and its achievement as the greatest achievement that there is.

Think about it. The Source set forth or achieved through Its conceptual understanding a plan which, because it is not sequential in the fullest sense, has already awakened each part of self to the fullest. This gets us into the "eternal now" space and it is a little difficult to understand, but try looking at the "eternal now" as a point of contact which the Creator and His Plan hold for you. This point of contact is the sense of achievement which shows you your truly unconditional and fully integrated state.

You can understand, then, that achievement is an inspirational point held by the Source in Its evolving understanding to motivate each of us to recognize the fully unlimited and heart-motivated basis from which to create.

4

Bridging

All of you know what a physical bridge looks like and you have experienced crossing one. You may not recognize, however, that bridges are built spiritually in a step-by-step manner. They are constructed in much the same way as a physical bridge is constructed. It takes first the understanding that a bridge is needed in order to begin the bridging process.

Now you might say that in the realization session a foundation is laid to further bridging or further understanding or connecting two aspects together so that a clearer understanding can be present. A good example is the constant bridging on many levels and in many ways that all of you are constructing in regard to the emotional body and the heart qualities and energy. In a realization session you may see certain events that you have accepted, creating certain patterns of behavior that limit, restrict or impact you or at least do not allow you to expand your life as you truly want. The realization session then begins to send out energy or begins to spin a web as a spider spins a web, which will connect various aspects of your emotional body into your heart.

Let me give you an example: a polarity relationship has just ended and you are feeling sadness and loss. In a realization session you may begin to realize that your partner and you made a choice that is probably for the best, that it is not an all-encompassing loss, that obviously you have had other relationships, so obviously you will have more. Perhaps your relationship partner still wishes to be a friend. Even if this is not true, the realization session shows you that the physical loss you are feeling can be helped through a spiritual bridging, a conceptual bridging, and this assists in allowing a clearer new foundation for relationships on the physical level.

Once the supportive framework or bridging process has been made mentally and spiritually, it is much easier for the emotional body and the physical body to make the connection. Indeed, your emotional body needs the inspiration of the spiritual perspective, and it needs the conceptual abilities and the logic of the mental body. It needs the support of the physical body in order to trust again what seems to it not always to be trustworthy. In other words, after ending a relationship you must he willing to try again, and it takes the bridging process to allow another level of contact to come into your life.

I have used the polarity area as an example, because for many of you this is an important key, and I refer you to several other chapters that talk about polarity. Bridging happens gradually. I refer you to chapter 34, "The Twilight Zone," to see that there is a process in building a bridge. It takes some time on the physical level to do that. It reaches a critical mass when there is more than 50% of the bridge built, and that is when most of you can trust the new level, because there is enough support built to approach that new level and therefore your trust can help you leap across what is yet unknown or unexplored.

Bridging increases the amount of creativity that you can allow to move through yourself. Say, for example, that you are a painter and are tired of the way you have been painting and you want to go into a whole new perspective of painting. You don't even know what it is but you know that you want to do it. You can feel that. There is a sense of connection, of knowingness. Now this is the spiritual body seeking to build a bridge to that newer, clearer, broader perspective of using your creativity. In order to be willing emotionally and physically to begin to utilize those abilities that your spiritual or soul level is projecting for you, a realization session is necessary where you explore conceptually your various potentialities for expressing this new level. You begin to build on that energy initiative that the spiritual has already started.

There needs to be an understanding that this bridging process can be scientifically approached or emulated from a Source-level perspective or viewpoint. There is nothing more organized, or-derly or structurally well designed than our Source and Its evolu-tion. It first puts forth a desire, and then It looks conceptually at what is desired and then chooses a creative potential or channel that invokes the emotional response or flow, which then builds the foundation and thus creates an all-encompassing bridging struc-ture to what has been desired. This bridging process is absolutely essential in order to realize and use your potential. Now the good news is that in every area in which you are seeking to be clearer

you have already built bridges, partially. You are not just beginning to construct them. All of you have bridges that are a quarter
or half or three quarters complete in all these areas. Or probably
for many of you the bridge is complete but you just haven't
connected the energy into crossing it, which is what the emotional
body does. So the emotional body is the key to allowing you to
use what has been constructed already. It may be all that is left of
a whole area that you have been trying to get in touch with but
haven't somehow been able to "turn on."

The emotions, when plugged in, flow the energy over the
structure that has been created conceptually and divinely inspired
and supported by the physical plane, or on the spiritual level by a
support base. There is no need to feel unworthy or to feel behind
in your evolution. All you have to do is contact all of these "works
in progress" or bridges that you are constructing, and as each area
is completed in a realization session and the emotional body
begins to energize them, your consciousness will flow into this
new level of understanding. It is an automatic process set up by
the Source Itself. Is it not exciting to see that? Truly it can be an
inspiration to see that you are not just leaping into the next level
but constructing a bridge into it all of the time. With every
communication that you make to everyone on every level you are
creating a bridging effect which literally is taking you to that next
level in every area. This section is meant to inspire you to show
you how well you are doing.

For many of you, as you connect the emotions in more clearly,
you are completing old bridges by allowing the energy to finally
flow on them and link you into an ever-clearer expression.

5

Feeling Buried or Overwhelmed

Many of you have come to physical existence not really wanting to be here. You have been persuaded by your teachers or by your own feeling of responsibility or love for humanity to come to Earth and help. Then when you came here you found yourself overwhelmed or "buried" in the third dimension.

There is for some a tremendous sense of restriction in being in the third dimension. The slowness of manifestation in physical existence irritates and frustrates many. Sequential time tends to throw one out of the focus of the eternal now, seems to place limitations on what can be done at any one time.

There is often a definite cocreator or group aspect to the feeling of overwhelm. If you experience headaches or discomfort in the solar plexus, there are often beliefs that you have to do it all yourself, your family expects it, your boss expects it, your groups expect it, the Creator expects it. You have the full responsibility to see that everything goes right. You must say "yes" to every request or you are negligent in your duty. This often comes from a life in a convent or ashram where you were dedicated to helping people and could not refuse help to anyone.

An overwhelm is often accompanied by a feeling of pressure and an effort to work over that pressure, which leads to anxiety which manifests in the solar plexus area or the assimilative area (digestive or elimination area).

This also affects the choice area where there is a feeling that you have no choice, must say "yes," feel forced into doing something you don't want to do. This sometimes causes trauma of some kind in the throat area — laryngitis, sore throat, coughing, etc.

This also ties into a feeling of guilt or unworthiness when you can't do it all no matter how hard you work.

Sometimes this brings forth an effort to escape from this overwhelming responsibility in many ways such as sleep, drugs, running away, etc.. The emotional body often rebels at this overwhelm. It feels that its needs are not being met and it puts up a lot of resistance and doesn't allow you to make good use of your time. You probably realize that, if you made good use of your time, you could accomplish all that you desire to do, but you are paralyzed by a flow of demand that seems to be unending.

Now, this overwhelm in your perception is brought on by the feeling that the Creator has given you this mission, that you must do this yourself, but you can't delegate any of this or it will not be done well enough. Or those in charge or humanity may have given you the overwhelming mission, and you have no recourse because they are so demanding.

There is within this topic the need to surrender and the fear or hesitation about surrendering to the Cosmic Plan. Remember you have only a piece of the Cosmic Plan to accomplish, you are not responsible for the whole Plan.

In many instances you feel no support from one or two of the bodies (mental, physical, emotional and spiritual). Then an overwhelm usually indicates that the consent of the four bodies has not been brought into the area you are working on. There is a rebellion in one or two of the bodies, most often the emotional body but sometimes the physical or mental.

View carefully when the overwhelm comes in. Is it when someone else is scheduling your time? That indicates a freedom aspect. Perhaps it is overwhelming when there is a lot of interaction with humanity necessary. It may be the communication area that is blocked.

The group/cocreator aspect is not open. Sometimes sequential time seems never enough, you can't fit it all in and don't recognize that you create your own time. It appears that you are stuck with or limited by the third dimension. What you can create is a flowing that is not limited by time; time then will fit into it rather than you having to fit into time.

Sometimes there is a feeling of being buried by the third dimension. The third dimension seems to bury or trap you in the Earth, stuck in the mud of the Earth. You believe that the Earth cannot be as spiritual as you are or desire to be. Any attachment you make on the Earth or to the Earth will trap you here, so you try to avoid communication with the Earth, avoid contact with that level. There are often past lives where you have been buried, sealed in caves, buried alive, etc. Remember that the physical, including the Earth, is just as spiritual, made of the same substance as the spiritual. It is operating at a slower frequency, greater density, but that doesn't make it less a part of the Creator. It is a privilege to experience in this the dense area. It is a boon to your evolution and allows you to see where you are. It mirrors where you are. When you are moving in the higher dimensions, it is difficult to look at yourself and see what your beliefs really are and what you are really creating. There is very slow evolutionary progress once you reach those higher levels, and so it behooves you to make that progress on the third dimension.

Many have chosen not to partake any further of the third dimension and some have not experienced it all. They have stayed in the fourth dimension and have been very, very slow at evolving, even though they had much less programming to work on than many of you here on Earth. Now is really your opportunity. As humanity moves from the third-dimensional operation to the fourth it doesn't mean that you give away the third-dimensional ability to see and to mirror. You have the best of both worlds right now as you come into the New Age, and I hope that you will take full advantage of it.

6

The "Shuddering Syndrome"

This may seem to be a strange title. I have used it to explain the process of adjusting from one level to the next. I refer you to the chapter on "Bridging" also. As you evolve and grow in your life perspective you may or may not recognize that your awareness is plugged into many levels of understanding simultaneously. This means, for example, that if you are in the sixth grade in school you may be reviewing some subjects that you did not understand completely in the fourth grade. You are certainly studying all of the sixth-grade subjects, but you may have begun a comprehensive study with the seventh-grade material, some of the eighth, and are beginning to delve into the ninth and reading about the tenth, and even considering the eleventh and twelfth grade material.

You are literally energizing the next few levels which you will comprehensively experience and grow into within the next two to four years in your evolution. And you are also reviewing those points which you haven't "got" yet. Now, you are all familiar with those points. Something will come up in your life and, as you understand more and more about old patterns of behavior, you may say, "I thought I had gotten rid of that one and here it comes sailing back into my life." Well, that is a review process of something that has spiraled around again to see if you have completely understood it. Now, if you have, you can look at it objectively with no attachments and no adverse effects and say to yourself, "Good, I really do understand that one this time." If, on the other hand, some of it is not entirely assimilated or understood or you still have some emotional attachments that get in the way or interfere in your complete acceptance of this situation, then you have an opportunity in your life to look again at this specific learning experience.

Also, of course, there are always new areas of understanding that will keep being available to you, and I have called these new areas the "shuddering syndrome." Well, I had to call it something, and I am looking vibrationally at how many of you contact a new area, and that's why I have named it that. Have you ever reached out tentatively to touch something, not quite sure how it would feel, and then you pulled back. Then as you pulled back you said, "No, I want to touch that." Perhaps several times you approached it and started to touch it only to back out again, and then with an effort you touched it and, lo and behold, it wasn't so bad after all. In point of fact it was a good contact and you accepted it much more completely than you thought you could. This back-and-forth movement in an opening into your awareness is a shudder, a vibrational shudder. It's almost like a dance, but the dance isn't secure, it has misgivings about where it wants to go. It has no sense of direction at this point of hesitancy in the contact.

Now, while this contact is not secure and you are dancing around in it without a sense of direction, what you usually get is confusion. "I don't know where I'm going, I'm not quite sure where I am, and what in the heck is going on anyway." You know that a door somewhere has opened. You can feel it but you don't know how to fully make contact with it, thus the back-and-forth shudder. Now, another reason I use the term "shudder" is that it is the emotional body that usually has some fears, or overwhelm, or insecurity in your ability to reach forth and grasp this opportunity. Actually it may not be an opportunity that you choose to use extensively, but you have to grasp it first to move into it and see what it is and understand it in order to have a choice as to how extensively you want to be involved in this new area. You may hesitate or move back and forth in the contact, not sure where the contact is. Now, you may make a contact and not recognize that you really energized a new opportunity, a new perspective that is trying to open you up.

Let's use the example of abundance. Many of you are seeking to allow in a more abundant flow. There may be at times an opportunity to actually be in association with others who have the means to bring in an abundant flow. You perhaps don't understand it fully yet or you've blocked that natural ability, and so the universe says to you, "As you are a cocreator I'll bring you an opportunity to cocreate with another who understands the abundance flow more completely." Now, let us say that you have some group programming or reluctance in the cocreator level. You still believe that it is important that you achieve your evolution by yourself, or there is another non-clear area that affects this opportunity. Someone may come to you then and say, "Why don't we do some things together," and you may not recognize that this is the Universe knocking at your door saying, "I understand that you want a more abundant flow. I've looked around and here is how you can have it. Associate with this clearer perspective that understands it and you can flow with it." Can you accept it? Many times your inability to accept partnerships and groups and alignment with others, with humanity, makes it difficult or makes you reluctant to surrender to the cocreator level. This is that shuddering syndrome.

Now you truly want to recognize your unlimitedness, everyone does, but how many of you can allow others to bring it to you? It is not a passive allowing, it is an active participation where you surrender to the process but grasp the opportunity or the opening that comes through the surrender and move into it. Generally speaking, it is your relationship with others on every level, not only the human level but also your relationship with the Hierarchy, the spiritual teachers and, in a very basic sense, your relationship with the Source and with the Source's Divine Plan that is involved.

Now, I have been seeking to assist in clearing the emotional body because I, Vywamus, feel that this is a vital part of your transformation, to have a clearer emotional perspective. There is a need to understand that you do not have to hold on to or grasp so tightly the current perspective that you now hold in your emotional body that you don't allow in the other cocreator perspective which would assist you to realize an ever-clearer perspective.

Let us look conceptually at the shuddering effect. If you see the Source as a circle, then within the circle there are unlimited points of light that are all blinking and twinkling at their own rate.

Each one has an individual vibration, but they are not incompatible with the overall vibration of our circle or the Source. But it isn't yet as finely attuned as it can be. Each light has a unique perspective which adds to the Whole. Each point of light represents one of us, the individualization process.

This represents the cocreator level. Each point of light, then, is seeking to align its vibration smoothly, evenly, into the divine rhythm of the Whole. If you look long enough at this circle through your third eye, what you will see is the shuddering effect. The movement of the individual perspective is not yet evenly attuned to the divine process. Certainly it has the potential to be as comprehensively balanced in its divine state as the overall Plan, the overall circle, but it is yet a baby cocreator, and each point of light shows through its vibration how completely attuned it is at this point.

Now, it is wonderful to behold a point of light within the Whole when it becomes fully aligned with the overall Plan or when it has accepted its full cocreator identity. It rather looks at first like a sun which has gone nova, and this tremendous expansion of light potential literally connects this point of light and its understanding with every other point of light in the circle. It becomes completely integrated. Every other point of light receives from this greatly expanded point more light, more balance, more understanding, more love, more gratitude, and, of course, it assists every other point of light in its balance. Can you see, then, that visually we can look at each cocreator and understand from its vibration how attuned, how evenly balanced it is. Now why is this important? Well, all of you are developing your clairvoyant abilities or seeking to, and you will want to look visually at the individualization process, its vibrational rate, and you may wonder why you suddenly see a flickering. This is the reason. New opportunities are coming into that particular point of light, and it is moving in and out trying to accept them.

Perhaps the most important point, and the reason I have done this chapter, is to show you that your emotional body with its learning is the absolute key for all of you. If your emotional body trusts an opening and enters it, then that shuddering settles down to a clearer perspective which is expanded through that connection, and the shuddering ceases. Your emotional body must accept opportunities first. Without its acceptance, generally speaking, there is too much resistance to utilize an opportunity fully. You may dance in and out of it, but you need the cooperation of your emotional body in order to use that opportunity comprehensively or even to make a balanced decision, a clear decision concerning as to whether or not you wish to use that opportunity. Because, of course, that is true. If someone knocks at your door selling something, you may or may not choose to use that opportunity, but the contact must be clear enough that you can decide if what the universe is bringing to your door is something that you desire to try.

7

Support of the Soul

The soul lends you its support in all of your activities. Sometimes you don't feel or notice that the soul is there or don't feel that it cares anything about you, but truly it is the aspect of self that is connected to the spiritual plane, to the divine, and it is always attempting to come through your personality, always attempting to come into your life and guide you toward your evolution. It is infinitely patient and seeks always to make the connection with you. What can stop it?

1. The belief that it isn't there, that there is no such guidance.

2. The feeling of being unworthy of the guidance.

3. A lack of trust in its ability to operate on the physical.

4. The focus into the ego/personality and its refusal to align with the Divine Will.

5. As a corollary to number four, the focus on the "comfort factor" and one's own needs and desires in third-dimensional existence.

The soul is always supportive, and the way to get in touch with it is to surrender to the heart. This is not the only way, but it is a good one. Surrender through your heart to the Divine Will. I have mentioned that many times in this book in various chapters. This will indeed bring in the soul, which will be channeling also your higher spiritual levels.

Another way is through a meditative state. Meditation almost always brings in the soul level. There are many ways to meditate:

1. Clearing and stilling your mind.
2. Focusing on a candle or another object.
3. Focusing on the Creator or the light.
4. Using guided visualization techniques.
5. Using sound or mantra.
6. You can also just focus on the soul and channel it. Ask for contact with the divine aspect of self.
7. If you are scientifically inclined, perhaps you can put yourself into an alpha state, in which your brain waves are approximately eight cycles per second, through biofeedback or a tape or your own experience of that state.
8. You can use a technique of watching the river of the mind go by and see the thoughts flowing by on it. Then as you feel yourself reach for one and start to consider it, put it back and allow the flow to go on. Don't engage in any of the thoughts.

How do you know when you are supported by the soul? You know the soul is working through you when everything is going well and all your needs are anticipated and provided for, when your mission in the Plan is flowing well in physical existence, when you are not running into blocks, lags, gaps and resistance of the body or emotions or resistances of the physical universe about you. Then you are allowing the soul to support you, to give you a feeling of security and worthiness.

The soul is the aspect of self that you can depend upon to help the other three bodies of the four-body system. It is especially useful when the mental and emotional bodies are in conflict, when you are trying to do something rationally and intelligently, and your emotional body is jumping up and down screaming. That is when you need to abandon the focus on both the mental and emotional and focus on the soul bringing its overview into the dispute. There is always a meeting ground that the soul can bring forth. You can do the same with the female and male polarities when they have trouble blending. The soul can help them through its aspect of unconditional love, through the heart chakra, to which the soul is connected directly. The soul can easily stimulate the heart chakra and vice versa.

So using the heart qualities stimulated by the soul will aid in these disputes, will bring you into an evenly balanced state. Many of you have had experience with a soul-merged state and you realize that you have this connection. Use it as often as you can. It is really the same connection that you use for channeling. It is an attunement to the spiritual level, and at that spiritual level you can contact your soul, the spiritual teachers or the angelic kingdom.

Make this attunement part of your daily routine in some way. Remember that all of your four bodies should be given an equal chance. For many of you your spiritual body or soul receives a very small amount of time compared with the other three. Love them all, enjoy them all. This is the purpose of life experience on the physical plane. This is the mirroring effect that you have come to Earth to use. It is the movie that you desired to make and have come to Earth to direct called, "This Is Your Life." It needs a director, and the soul is the one, the best one. Believe me when I say that the soul has all of the qualifications for this position and it can utilize the other bodies in the most favorable, satisfying and productive way that you desire and have invoked.

8

Joining the Multiplicities of Self

As you understand by now, you are a multileveled, multifaceted being. Perhaps there are more levels than you can yet imagine, more aspects that at this point in your evolution are seeking to be integrated or realized. This is an extremely important point in evolution, for you personally, for the Earth, and certainly, in my opinion, for the overall Sourceness which we are a part of. It is truly an exciting period, one in which communication, whether we talk about it as a link of two specific human beings or a link of all multiplicities or aspects of self, is very important.

The self, of course, is part of the Source in its linkage system as it manifests from what one could call the God-head, spreading and radiating and exploring. It literally expands through explosive points that are generated through the overall conscious awareness of its own truth.

Bringing that down to Earth so that we may look at it, although that is not "an Earthy subject," we can see that each of you at this time is exploring the physical, emotional, mental and spiritual perspectives in order to understand and communicate with them in a way that allows a resolution, a clearer point of view, an acceptance of the purposes for which you have come forth on the Earth.

Now, I've said to many of you over and over again that your soul does not have just one purpose. It has an unfolding or a focus of purpose which expands, each point expanding from the point that has gone before. Thus, as you begin to understand one purpose, from that understanding comes forth the next point of your purposes which you will contact and flow within.

Now, you have what I will call a divine pattern or blueprint at the soul level. And this can be looked at as energy; it can also be looked at as purpose. It can also be looked at as an ideal way to put all of your multifaceted perspectives and levels together. There is not just one ideal, although in an energy sense there is possibly one clearest perspective. But how you reach that perspective is multifaceted or is a journey of exploring and going all around that ideal until you finally accept it.

Let's say for example, that you've always wanted to build a house. You knew from the time you were a child that you would build your own house. And I mean you would build it. You would put it up brick by brick, or board by board, you would build a house yourself. Now you grew up with this in the back of your mind, and let us say you learned all the skills; they seemed to come very easily and you knew your house would be built by you.

Now you also had various sets of blueprints and were looking for the right one. You would draw a sketch for your house and you would say, "No, that's not quite it." And you would draw another sketch of your house and make changes, and somehow it never seemed to be exactly the right one. Then let us say you married. Let us say you were male and your wife was eager and interested in helping you build your house. She had her own unique skills that she brought to the project. She knew exactly how to change the plan that you were not quite satisfied with, make just those small changes so that the plan was exactly that ideal that you desired.

Now you were both very satisfied with this plan. It seemed exactly the structure in which you wanted to live. And thus you began to build the house. Together you had selected and found a piece of land that seemed exactly right. It was a focus on which you could now build that ideal, you could allow it to manifest within this particular point on the Earth. It went well. You built it and each step was fun, you enjoyed it. Perhaps sometimes it took a little longer than you expected, perhaps sometimes you had to change a few things, but finally you got your house built. Your wife did her part, helping you build it, then furnishing it, so it really became a joint effort. And now your house stands complete, furnished, just exactly the way you wanted it. And the two of you move into your house.

Now, what you will deal with at that time is beliefs concerned with when the blueprint is manifest on the Earth—what then? What will you do when the house is complete? For some there may be a loss. You've become so involved with the house that you don't see that the house itself is simply a prelude to a greater purpose that can now be realized.

One such purpose might be that you and your wife would have children who would live in this house. Your creativity would grow within this house. And perhaps, because the house is your ideal, it allows you to have a place of balance, a place of peace, a place of tranquillity. And from that more balanced perspective you go forth within your purposes more secure, because that creative base and a link to it have been established.

By now you recognize that it is not necessarily a physical house but a creative base that both your male and female polarity have created together, so that your growing creativity can expand when that feels complete enough. Then your purposes will manifest. Now, keep in mind this is really a birth point. It is a birth focus upon which everything else can then be based. It is a foundation. And for many of you it has been called the birth of the Christ within. Some religions call it being born again. Others may say you have made a link to the soul through a recognition of a foundation for the soul's purpose on the Earth. There needs to become manifest, then, a foundation of understanding which you have constructed yourself. You must build it piece by piece or link by link.

I refer you in this chapter to the chapter called "Earth Link — Trial and Error," explaining how you can link up all aspects, all points of view, brick by brick, board by board, nail by nail, point by point. Then, you create a linkage system within your Earth focus or Earth perspective which is that ideal blueprinting of the soul on the Earth.

Another way of saying it is that you allow or accept that point of contact with the soul which holds your divine blueprint. It's a process of allowing that level by level. There is an important point where it becomes strong enough to be called a soul-merge, meaning that there is enough of that soul present that it overlights the personality level so much that the personality level begins to accept direction from the soul.

This multifaceted approach, then, to existence on the physical level begins to attract other aspects of yourself. For many of you right now on the Earth what is going on is that this soul link is becoming so strong that other aspects or units of soulness, if you will, are joining, or coming to focus with the Earth connection that has already been made. It's like having a channel which will receive the electrical energy of the soul, and because it is open enough you are able to bring in more electrical energy of the soul which has not seemed available to the Earth before. You are linking other levels of self into the process.

Let me share this with you. We could look at your galactic level as a core point within your soul's growth or unfoldment. We could say the galactic core is that particular level where the soul is headquartered. A level beyond that is what we might call the universal level. It's really more of a monadic level or at least the beginning of that monadic expression. So the aspects of your soul are gathered at the galactic core.

In other material I talked about the fact that the Earth is now open to communication at the galactic core level. It has made a contact there. There is another chapter in this material called "The Galactic Connection" and I refer you to that. But the point is that you have at least 12 souls, we could divide it differently and see it as 24 also. We have then a multifaceted soul-aspected perspective which gathers or unites or integrates at the galactic core. Now, because you are on the Earth as a soul, you are more open because the Earth is more open to communicate with the galactic level. You are joining or uniting with the aspects of the soul that have not yet been a part of your Earth experience but are contacted at that galactic level. The energy of such aspects is beginning to flow electrically into that focus of the soul that has guided your life on the Earth. This is the electrical stimulation that all of you are feeling. It comes through your Planetary Logos, Sanat Kumara, and it is filtered then through this soul perspective.

The multifaceted soul, then, is able to draw on the various aspects which have gone forth and have expressed within certain dimensions or points of view. You are familiar with the third-dimension expression because you are currently focused there. But there are other aspects of you which are focused fourth-, fifth-, and sixth-dimensionally, that have a point of view almost exactly like your third-dimensional focus. This is sometimes confusing for many of you. The book *Scopes of Dimensions* seeks to show you how to bring these points of view together.

The uniting factor is the galactic connection, the divine blueprint, you might say, that your particular soul's aspect is mirroring now into physical existence. The divine blueprint that you are building on the Earth is a mirroring or a reflection of that more comprehensive point of view at the galactic core. But because of the Harmonic Convergence, all of what the galactic core represents, that comprehensive multi-faceted point of view of who you are, is now being drawn to the Earth and drawn from what you have learned on the Earth. There is a reciprocal flow and exchange from the galactic core for many of you. It has intensified your life. There is more soul direction. Much more. There has been more since April 15th, 1989. And of course, there will be other points later which are a part of the Earth's evolution. And each time the Earth opens to a clearer perspective concerning who it is, you benefit, and you step up in the evolutionary scale and then are able to contact that galactic core more directly.

So we have here the physical Earth-level perspective, which for many of your lives was guided by a personality level. We have also a soul's perspective that you are in the process of integrating to be a guidance of this personality level. And then we have the galactic core which is headquarters for a more comprehensive or a more widely aspected use of the soul than you have yet contacted. We have then a universal guidance system beyond the galactic core which, my friend, is still a part of what directs what I might call physicality.

When we go to the universal level, we have only reached the doorway to physicality, the doorway beyond which your spiritual perspective is not a part of physical existence. Truly about nine-tenths of your potentiality lies beyond physical existence.

On a piece of paper you can draw ten horizontal lines that are about an inch apart. The bottom inch is physical existence. If we enlarge that bottom inch see that it is divided into four parts, one-fourth inch each. The first one-fourth inch is the personality, the next one-fourth represents the part of the soul you have recognized and is now being integrated, the third one-fourth inch will be the galactic core level of your soul connection. The fourth one-fourth is the universal level which guides that whole inch we have called physicality.

Can you see then that previously you have been exploring one-fourth of one inch? You are now exploring one-half of one inch and are beginning to explore three-fourths of one inch; you have yet to explore the full inch, which will lead you to explore the other nine inches in existence.

Now, in order to show you who you really are, if you look at the scale the other way, the top inch represents your monadic exploration. And there truly is a light connection, an energy flow from that monadic level down into the inch that you are exploring on the physical level. Now, certainly I could give many ways to view this. In *The Source Adventure* I've looked at it a little differently, and I refer you to that material. But my point is that there are areas, aspects, multiplicities of self that you have not yet dreamed of from your physical focus.

It is wondrous to know and look forward to a point of evolution where you will explore the other nine-tenths because, my friends, it will be done without struggle, without pain, without resistance. This point that we have called the bottom inch is the focus, the period where you get rid of such resistances, and thus you can flow freely, dance creatively, joyously, harmoniously on the rest of the trip. It is wondrous to know that the Plan has included the means for helping everyone at the point called physical existence to resolve the misperceptions, to let go of the struggle. Then, although the learning is eternal beyond that inch, it is not a struggle, it is an exercise in creative stretches in realization that raise you to the heights, in a joyous process for which you searched and dreamed.

Built into the Plan, then, is a longing to contact that part of you that understands how to evolve without struggle. And, my friends, you are coming closer and closer to that point. Indeed, at the point of ascension you begin to realize through that last quarter of an inch of exploration what lies beyond the universal perception that you have envisioned. I say to you, "Look forward to stepping into that universal expression, but note that what you consider to be universal still only leads you to one-tenth of what you are destined to explore." If that seems to put a limitation on it, that is not my intent; it is simply showing you that the process expands eternally, and you have the wondrous prospect to look forward to of unlimited expansion within it.

This time and place is for releasing resistances to the integration of the multiplicities of self. As each one brings you its resistances you can handle them, and thus integration can take place.

9

Avoidance Programming

What are you trying to avoid? Well, usually it is something you are afraid of, not comfortable with, don't like, feel that you can't do well, are bored with or feel will lead you into responsibilities or experiences for which you are not prepared.

Avoidance programming is often connected with addiction. One takes up an addictive habit to escape from or avoid something. In fact, one way to look at what you are avoiding is to notice at what time or in what situation you find it necessary to indulge in your favorite addiction, be it alcohol, drugs, eating, TV, sex, movies or anything that you use in an out-of-control fashion for the purpose of relaxing or shutting out the world.

Now, addiction is one way of avoidance, another is holding on to an old pattern and not allowing anything new into your life, and that way you avoid the discomfort and sometimes confusion, mistakes or mis-communications that result from venturing into something new.

Adopting new patterns, procedures, ways of operation test your awareness, your communication abilities, your ingenuity, your creativity and your balance to the limit sometimes, and many are not ready for that. It is especially true that people have a limit to the number of new experiences that they can cope with. That is why it is wise to hold on to a few possibly boring duties such as doing the dishes or mowing the lawn to keep something traditional that you are familiar with and for which you don't have to build a new procedure. Thus you can avoid having to face new decisions on every level at every time of the day.

Now, some can handle this and more. They look for adventure and excitement and new experiences, but others, and that is most, can only handle a certain dosage, and your subconscious will tell you by putting up a great deal of resistance as you try to move into something that is outside your limit.

I believe that the best use of the avoidance pattern (and it is occasionally useful) is to protect yourself from an overwhelm or overburden of new experiences at any one time. You do know when it is getting to be too much, when you have more stress than you can cope with, and in that case a little avoidance, a healthy escape to a more stress-free environment or situation is a reasonable choice.

The best way to handle this overwhelm, of course, is to attempt to bring your body back into balance through handling the energy, seeing all the chakras open, meditation, moving into alpha, going for a walk, exercising, a social encounter with friends. These work much better than most of your addictive patterns, with the advantage that you don't have to break the habits later.

Be sure also to look at what you are avoiding, not just the particular action but the perspective, the overall results that particular activity would bring forth, and work with clearing any fear of that.

Allow yourself to accept your joyous child aspect, let that guide you through the heart in avoiding what is becoming an overwhelm without bringing in something which you will later need to handle.

10

Earth Link — Trial and Error

In order to understand the above title it is necessary to look at the Cosmic Plan and to see the part that physical existence plays within it. The Earth represents a specific focus within physicality which all of you have chosen in order to help the Plan evolve.

Truly, your being here is not personal. You can view it personally and learn from it. But the Cosmic Plan itself is evolving through this aspect which is called the Earth. Now, I have written in several other books about the fact that the Plan moves or spirals or evolves and that there really is not a fixed or predestined point which it is reaching, unless you consider unlimitedness to be a predestined point. What I am saying is, the Source begins a Cosmic Day, and I refer you to the book *The Source Adventure* to understand that particular premise more completely. But it sets up, literally, a framework or a support system through which to explore a particular theme, the theme being "courage" on this

Cosmic Day. Now the Source potentially knows all there is to know about courage. But It sets up the specific framework and then evolves through the exploration within this framework. One of the points in which Its evolution takes place has been called physical existence. It literally is a point of magnification which shows the Source how well It's doing.

Now, if we bring this down to the Earth level, we can see that you as a soul and also, of course, an aspect of Source, have come to the Earth to view your creativity, using what we might call the "trial-and-error" method. In a life you may seek to be a doctor. Perhaps the circumstances of your birth and family seem to make this difficult, and what you learn is alternative ways of bringing in a goal, whether it is, as in our example, becoming a doctor, or any other goal that you have chosen on the Earth. If, in your many lives, certain patterns of behavior seem to wipe out reaching a goal or keep you from having what you are seeking, then through the realization process that this book is discussing you can see more clearly what needs to be realized about yourself.

The trial-and-error method within the Earth's third-dimensional focus has led you to explore extensively over an average of 1800 to 2000 lives — some of you less, some of you more. Because of the nature of the third dimension as a "turn-around-point" or the process where involution becomes evolution, there is again within you a process that, in this book, we are calling "realization" going on. What it really means is allowing a clearer understanding of how things fit together, rather than simply repeating experiences over and over from the same point of view.

Now, if you are cooking something which needs to be mixed or blended well, there may be certain ingredients which seem resistive to the stirring process and you get some lumps in the mixing process. You have to keep mixing it and stirring it until those lumps dissolve. The movement, then, of the fourth dimension is the means to dissolve crystallization or lumps that have occurred in your living in the third dimension.

Now, the fourth dimension, as used in the realization process, is often a visual contact or a visualization that allows you to see how your spiritual, emotional, mental and physical perspectives can come together. You may see a resistive point or conceptually understand it. Then the fourth-dimensional flow can, by stirring up these perspectives and seeing where the "lumps" or crystallized points are, keep moving the area until it comes together and is integrated.

This is truly the purpose of physical existence. It first brings you a particular focus or what we might call a multiplicity of focuses within a larger focus, which is the Earth perspective itself. By that I mean you have a physical body focus, your own personal focus, within the larger overall Earth focus. You have an emotional perspective, a mental perspective or focus and certainly your soul's spiritual perspective or focus. Now, there are many levels of blending and I refer you to the chapter in this book called "Joining the Multiplicities of Self" in order that we may see more specifically all the levels that are being blended and joined together. But your purpose here on the Earth is as a focus or aspect of Source that is being blended or stirred within a larger focus or aspect of Source.

Thus you are learning to blend into the overall human scene, but at the same time learning to blend into the overall soul scene, whose purposes have brought you to the Earth. And so on, and so on, level by level, until we see Source level or focus itself. Now, that does not mean that the Earth is not a focus of Source. But we could look at it as a jointed telescope, in which, as you open it, one level comes out from another.

I am seeking to convey, then, that the Source unfolds Itself level by level until It has reached a point called the third dimension. At this time It begins to, in Its conscious awareness, integrate all of what has been unfolded and explored in a step-by-step process back to the original point or premise. Thus It completes the loop or the spiral and allows the next level to be undertaken. The reason I've called this chapter "Earth Link — Trial and Error" is that on the Earth it is necessary or a part of the Plan for you to send out multiplicities of self in many ways in order that you will have explored so completely that every point of view can then be joined together. Now, is it necessary for you to experience everything? No, it is not. But it must be complete enough that, when you begin to integrate, there are points or focuses from a particular area which you have experienced that can then come back together. You probably will have had lives as a doctor, as a nurse, as a historian, as a philosopher, as a runner or an athlete, as a musician, as a poet, as a scientist, as a leader, as an organizer, as a business man, as a gardener, as someone that nurtures the Earth, as someone that nurtures humanity, as someone that nurtures the animal kingdom, and certainly many times as a nurturer of the aspect called Source Itself or the spiritual point of view.

You literally are on the Earth a nurturer. Each one helps the Source absorb or understand or know something from the particular embodiment which you have chosen in that life. There is never a waste, never a life not worthwhile. Yes, from a personal soul perspective there may be a sense of your life not being as widely scoped as you would like, or there is illness there and you wish that you did not have to go through that. But in the overall sense I am going to tell you something surprising. The Source does not notice illness, It does not notice blocks, It does not notice crystallization, not in the sense that it abstracts or blocks the learning process. Yes, the Source in Its allowingness and compassion sees Its aspects on the physical level sometimes struggle, sometimes create in a difficult manner. But It learns, It grows, It understands, It accepts all of what you have experienced, and all of what you are learning, and all of what you are realizing. It does not judge. It does not feel blocked because of your struggles. It accepts and appreciates what you are and what you are doing. It knows that you are growing and that the wisdom that is coming is a widely scoped wisdom indeed, because it is the wisdom of the experience of all of the Earth.

That is learning that comes through you. Or we could say that you are learning to accept. Thus truly the Earth link, the trial and error, is literally the process of the Source's evolution and each one of us expresses more and more completely the clear level of understanding that is available to us through the overall Earth link or what I have termed the mass-consciousness. Available to you through this mass-consciousness is the whole experience of Sourceness. All of what humanity and the other kingdoms have expressed on the Earth is stored there. That is available to you, not as an impactful part of you, not at all, but as an experiencing mode. Going back to that example of becoming a doctor where it didn't work out for you to become a doctor, let us say you never again on the Earth sought to become a doctor. You can, let us say, link that doctor aspect within your overall integration or system by delving into the mass-consciousness storing system, or what we call the Akashic Records. Not only will you find there your personal records but the records of all of humanity as they learn doctoring.

Now, can you read all that yourself at this point? Probably not, but know that I or other teachers or certain members of the Angelic Kingdom are delighted to help you to understand through all of the experiencing modes, all of the trial and error. The error is not a mistake — it is an experience that is not perhaps as clear as it can be. The ability to try and then allow that experience to become a focus by which the learning becomes ever clearer is important, and you've done that over and over on the Earth.

Now, for most of you, instead of contacting the trial and error on the third dimension, what becomes available to you is the fourth-dimensional flow, and you may access this through our help. The experiencing mode of the Akasha of the mass-consciousness can be contacted and you can then learn how to use it to resolve any sticky or unblended or stuck issues, what I earlier called lumps or crystallization. The realization process is the means to put it all together, and I say to you, it can allow your Earth focus, which has been third-dimensional until now, flow fourth-dimensionally and blend together into the clearest perspective that you have ever had. This will allow you to create a totally integrated point of focus for yourself and the Source which is called the point of ascension.

11

Unconditional Love

Unconditional love is very simple because it centers and brings to one point all of existence. Everything exists because of unconditional love. It is, then, the generative core from which existence flows. We could call it a fountain. We can call it a flow. We can call it many things, but it certainly is a basis upon which everything else exists. Over and over again you have heard us, your spiritual teachers, talk about unconditional love. And you have felt unconditional love. But you have felt it in many ways, from many points of view. And sometimes this is confusing. You have heard about it and not only felt it, but been told that it was your goal. It is your goal to utilize it.

Unconditional love is therefore a "charged" subject. It takes you into deep places in your consciousness. It mixes manifestation with the Source-level relationship which you have. It seeks to unite you, putting together all aspects of self so they fit together well and are not judgmental. But unconditional love is a flow and some of you are yet blocking that flow.

When you have realized the power and felt within you the free flowingness of unconditional love, it helps you generate contact with others communicatively. It shows you there are no differences at all in existence, that you and others fit together in your divine connection. Literally, then, unconditional love is the blending, merging and integrating aspect of yourself. Your love base is as unconditional as you can recognize at this point.

Some of you have opened your heart in a manner which brings recognition of others' strengths, of others' abilities. You recognize and appreciate them. This is an aspect of unconditional love which everyone is looking for. At the same time you may not be willing to internalize that unconditional love or turn it on yourself. Perhaps you do not see unconditionally your own strength and abilities. Unconditional love can be erased through a judgment factor. For many of you that judgment is more of yourself than others. Some of you have this judgment quality in both places, but literally all of you yet have some of it about yourself. Certainly unconditional love can erase or help heal self-judgment. Self-judgment is within you because you have not yet seen the beauty of who you are. And unconditional love sees beauty and perhaps focuses on it. It sees the strength of the divine. It allows contact with divine beingness in a nonjudgmental manner. Now, certainly discernment is an area which I have emphasized a great deal.

Unconditional love does not mean becoming a sacrifice or a victim. Unconditional love is very much a part of allowingness, and allowingness is balanced with discernment. I often use the example that, if someone is grinding his heel into your toe, you do not have to allow it. Your clearest action would be to pull your toe back from his heel, and let him continue to grind if he so chooses. Meaning that your allowingness of others should be balanced with discernment which states, "Others' non-clear perspectives do not need to impact or victimize me."

At the basic level of unconditional love there is no martyrdom. The Source does not victimize or create martyrs. But some of you are not sure subconsciously about that. In this material I have talked frequently about the Source-level relationship, stating that when you entered the individualization process, many of you felt less comprehensively in touch with the divine. Meaning that in the womb-like-state you seemed fully in contact with it, fully supported by it, fully conscious of it. It was like going from an awareness of a whole pie to an awareness of one slice of a pie.

Now, because the Creator had asked you to enter this individualized state, you, in your unconditional love for the Source and the realization that it was the next step for you in your evolution, agreed to do so. Now, many of you had expectations of what would come of that. The Creator had assured you that this was truly an unlimited state. Perhaps then you did not read the fine print which stated that you would realize this unlimitedness through your association with the cocreator level or with others. Thus when you seemed to be limited, you felt victimized, martyred or betrayed, and you immediately buried that response, because one does not allow such an emotion within oneself in regard to the Source or Creator, does one?

Well, in my opinion, such limiting emotions or beliefs must be pulled out and looked at, must be shifted into a clearer expression which then becomes an unconditional love response. Love cannot be limited. If you try to limit love, it becomes literally something besides unconditional love. Now, that may sound obvious. But for many of you in seeking your expression of unconditional love you go so far with it, and then you say, "That's all there is. There isn't any more. I can't go any further with this feeling, with this expression." And it is almost always the case that it is the Source-level relationship that needs to be explored in order to bring in finally the Source-level unconditional love.

No one, and I repeat, no one on the Earth, is yet capable of understanding love that is completely unconditional. All of you have put some strings on it. But this is part of your development and your evolution. It is also the freedom that you are seeking. Now, freedom may be looked at in many ways. And you will find it discussed in this material. But basically your freedom can be realized through unconditional love. When you are truly free, then the unconditionalness of love has room to express through you. It does not have obstacles in the freedom area which keep bouncing the love back, putting conditions on it.

Now, think about yourself in a relationship. You seek to be loving and harmonious. Many of you, though, say to your partner, "But what about me, my needs are not being met here." Now, I hasten to reiterate that you are not here to be a victim or a martyr to a love relationship. But I am emphasizing that unconditional love, when it is felt strongly enough, brings back to you from others an unconditional love response. So if the universe brings to you in the love area something that seems to limit or restrict you, this shows you that you have not yet allowed your love to become unconditional. Now, this is not a criticism. It is simply a way of seeing that the mirroring set up by the Creator works. When the mirror or a reflection from others brings an unconditional response back to you and you can accept it and recognize it, then you will know that your love has become truly unconditional, at least in that one situation.

There will ever be a journey of making all aspects of love unconditional. Now this is a vast subject, and I could write ten books on it. In point of fact there have been so many books written on love, they are almost unlimited, imagine that. And this is one area that your head can read about and absorb some information about. But your emotional body and your heart have to experience the love in order for it to be real to you. You will reach a point, and many of you have reached this already, where your heart is more than 50% open. Because of a critical-mass factor, then, you feel more connected through love than you feel closed or victimized by the process. There is a gradual unfoldment of the love center. And this is perhaps the most balanced way to express more and more unconditional love. Gradually, one step at a time through realizations in every area of your life, you take out each limitation. Each time you let go of a perspective of limitation you bringing a perspective of unconditional expression which is the same thing, my friends, as unconditional love. Indeed, when the Source invited you to swim in existence, invited you to do it without strings, without any barriers, this was an expression of unconditional love.

Unconditional love motivates the purpose area. When love is expressed unconditionally it must share. There is no question but that unconditional love spills over into all of the universe. It wants to help. It wants to share. It wants to express joy. It is eager to understand all points of view. It is patient and allowing, it is grateful for the privilege of being a part of existence. It takes out barriers. It creates the excitement of connecting with all possibilities. It allows the future to be virtually unlimited, the past to be forgiven, and the present to be a joyous adventure which is constantly unfolding.

12

Joy

I like to think of joy as the effervescent bubbles in creation. That's what keeps bursting forth through the creative process, much as the liquid of effervescent drinks keeps bursting to the surface. Now, many of you don't recognize it very often. Just occasionally do you allow the joy to surface and burst forth. But it is there, a part of your creative core. Certainly it is there, because, in my opinion, it is the basic motivator in existence itself.

Joy, of course, is a quality of the heart, and it only can be present when the heart is open enough to acknowledge it. Now, in an energy sense, the act of being joyful creates a surge of energy which connects with others in your environment, and they respond to this joy that is literally bubbling up and bursting out all over. If you think back to a time when you were with someone who was very joyful, or you were very joyful and with others, you will recall that joy can be very contagious, that it spreads rather easily and rapidly. Joy needs to be real in order to allow that effervescence. You can't fake it. Now effervescence, in an energy sense, is an electric effect which creates surges of energy which then defuse and spread out so that it may be easily integrated. Joy, then, is for the purpose of allowing integration, and it is necessary to use it to be fully integrated. It is a tool of the integrative process within Source.

Now, you may say to me, "I just can't be joyful all the time, even though I try." You are right, sometimes when you try to be joyful, what you get is not joy but an imitation which is not the same. Joy must be allowed, and its allowingness is brought forth or contacted through relaxation, through allowing yourself to release all sense of pressure or burden. It must come through a relaxed emotional body. If there is too much stress emotionally in your life, there is no way to allow that effervescent joy to come to the surface enough so that you can recognize it. You cannot be tense and joyful at the same time.

Joy is often contacted through the child within, and I refer you to the material in chapter 26. Joy is often connected to wonder – the appreciation and wonder that one has about existence, about the Creator, about the Plan, about other people and about the opportunity to express within the Plan. Joy allows movement, and it is the specific within creation that motivates participation within the Plan. Through it one acknowledges and recognizes one's part in the Plan. Through it other heart qualities begin to open and come forth.

Certainly, unconditional love, as described in the previous chapter, is stimulated through joy, and you could say unconditional love stimulates joy also. There is a good exchange. But perhaps joy is the effervescence which stimulates the unconditional love or allows it to integrate into the radiant core, which is that full integrator in existence.

Now, there is a difference between joy and what I call glee. Glee is not the same thing at all. It is a much less clear level. Mirth is not quite the same either. Glee laughs at others' discomforts, at their pain, at their difficulties. Mirth can appreciate the person, it sometimes laughs at itself, which is not bad. But joy is the full appreciation of everything that exists and a desire rather completely to play with everything. You know a small child, whether it is a human child or within the animal kingdom, always wants to play. They are truly joyful in their play. They want to play in existence. They want to enjoy it. There is that joy that bubbles up, and they enjoy being together in rolling and playing, and the movement that they create through their interaction is called evolution. Two puppies that are rolling together are learning something important. They are learning to get along with others. They are learning to be friendly and joyous without hurting one another or allowing themselves to be hurt. They are learning all about communication. So joy is therefore a basic foundation of clear communication; without it communication is never clear.

Now, some mental people bury their emotions, they don't acknowledge them, but sometimes there is an attempt, through an aspect of joy, to bring out the emotions. It is not a fully realized state of joy, but it is partially successful in that it becomes a stabilizing factor for those who are very mentally focused and don't recognize emotions very much at all. At least they have this partial acknowledgment through the heart that is joyous.

Now, that partial acknowledgment of joy is both a stabilizer and a stimulator. One is never content with it. There is always more sought, because at a basic level that being recognizes that joy is leading them to a more complete understanding. Now, this can be rather like a polarity split in the emotional area for them; the buried emotions try to use that joy as a ladder to climb out on, but because the very mental person has always buried emotions, they are not allowed out because they are not perhaps positive. The only area that is allowed to surface, because it comes more from a mental perspective, is anxiety. So you could say anxiety "reigns as king for a while" within those that are opening to joy but not yet allowing the emotions that are considered by the mental body and the subconscious to be negative to surface. You see, anxiety is one of the most — I'm going to use the term — difficult and destructive of all emotions, and it is because it has been reframed from an emotion into a mental perspective that becomes a prison for the one who is mentally focused. They are imprisoned between their desire to have this joy that they have been glimpsing, and the anxiety patterning which keeps reestablishing itself when they attempt to allow out the desired emotions.

Sometimes, particularly with those that are very mentally focused, unconditional love, compassion, and particularly trust are literally imprisoned beneath emotions which have been buried, such as distrust, limited love or what I would call the polarity opposite of all of the positive emotions which we equate with the heart. Therefore the very fact that they are more joyful stimulates a polarity split into anxiety, which keeps reinforcing, because they have buried the emotions, the imprisoned state of the other qualities of the heart. Now this is important information for those that are very mentally focused, and it is an important key to releasing the imprisoned heart qualities. For someone who sees life through their emotions, becoming more joyful can do several things. It inspires the emotions. But it also may create a sense of hopelessness, because a deep sense of unworthiness can come from this contact with joy. It says, there is the goal, but somehow I am not ever worthy to be that joyful, I might as well give up. In point of fact, that joy can change into a sense of hopelessness and pressure if, let's say, constant progress is not seen in opening up that joy area. It becomes then literally an emotional swing back and forth, positive and then, what you call negative, positive and negative, positive and negative, until one gets into that sense of hopelessness: "There is no way that I can ever remain focused where I want to be within the positive emotions through the heart area."

What needs to be done in both the cases of the mental focus and the emotional focus is to use joy as much as it is available. But not force it. Use it, enjoy it, be aware of it and communicate with it daily, invite it in in the morning. You might say, "I'm ready, how much joy is there for me today?" Then accept what comes. But say to yourself, "I'll be open to receiving more today. If I am ready, then I am ready. If my quota of joy seems small today, then I will look deeply within myself and see why. I will not pressure myself with 'shoulds.' I will not make myself feel unworthy because my cup of joy seems small today. I will instead allow what emotions are there — fear, or unworthiness, or whatever they are — to lead me ever deeper into understanding myself, so that I can allow that very basic joy to burst forth. I will seek to realize that the joy will never go away. My attunement to it may be less than I am fully capable of at any one moment, but I am growing in joy-awareness, and even if I cannot always see it, I know that that is true." By approaching the joy area in this manner I know that joy will "sneak up on you" and then you can enjoy without feeling pressured.

13

Free Flow

All of you are learning to "flow" in your life. And what that simply means is to allow the Divine to utilize you in a manner which is fully communicative to others and to all aspects within self. Now, that may be a little different interpretation of free flow than you have perhaps looked at before. If you are seeking to learn to swim, there are times when it is important to jump in the water and practice your swimming – allowing your body, your divine vehicle, to become comfortable with movement, to facilitate the movement in as rhythmic, smooth, and clear a manner as possible.

There are times, however, in which to sit quietly and envision all of what you wish to see in the swimming area. In other words, to see yourself swimming just exactly as you want to swim. Now, this is allowing yourself to begin to enter the free flow from the key point between the fifth and fourth dimensions. The fifth dimension is an area of understanding conceptually, of building a concept so clearly that it hooks into the Source-level ideal. Once it has so connected, it will flow more freely. The visualizations, then, that you do in any area to obtain or to bring in your goals are important. They can begin the connection into the free flow. If you jump into the water without any sort of concept as to why you are in the water or what your goal is, you will do a lot of fishing around before you begin to discover the way. Why not learn to bring the key with you, and then your vehicle within the free flow can utilize it to connect in fully?

Many of you are seeking to understand and connect with the area of free-flowing abundance, actually abundance in free flow or Sourceness — there is no difference. But perhaps you might see bringing in money as a specific within the free flow. In order to have an abundant flow one must then key in for the universe the concept of how to connect with this specific aspect of the free flow. Certainly we would like to suggest that your goal is probably to have free flow in all areas, not just money, but because you have come to the Earth and have literally taken apart your creativity, it is necessary to put it back together very specifically in each aspect of your life in order to have it flow freely. Now, existence is not without purpose. So to obtain an abundance from the universe, connecting in with the basic purpose for which you wish abundance can be helpful. Certainly I am not saying that the universe won't give you abundance if you want it for incidentals or for expenses. But I am telling you that basically abundance flows for the purpose of evolving the Plan. Therefore, the clearer you are on what part you play in the Plan, the more you see yourself involved in helping others and them helping you, the more comprehensively you sense your purposes connected into humanity over all evolution, the more your request will enter the basic level of creation and will come back to you abundantly.

Now, that is a simplification of the whole area of abundance, because if an individual, or a group perhaps, invokes abundance, they will certainly get it one way or the other, but they may not for a while be able to specifically see how it is coming in. In other words, perhaps the mail man does not deliver a check for a million dollars right away. Of course, that is possible eventually, too. But perhaps more people come into the group, or, in an individual case, an opportunity may come in to recognize more fully the qualities of the heart. What the universe will give you generally is the means to keep connecting into how to be ever more specific in your understanding of abundance. When you begin working on abundance, it may seem for a while that you are becoming more blocked in that area. You may have stimulated resistance and not be flowing freely due to the blocks that you have set up subconsciously.

Whether you are an individual or a group, until you can allow the abundance you are seeking, free flow is the plan that shows you step by step the means to accept your unlimitedness. But it flows through rock-city, if you will, or those areas where the blocks are that you need to recognize and remove.

I think all of you would like to bring in full abundance now — have all of the money that you have envisioned and all of the qualities of self flowing freely. I say to you, however, not meaning it as a criticism, but simply a comment, that it is important to step into the full abundance area gradually, otherwise it is like suddenly having a delivery of 10,000 opportunities, and you have not the faintest idea where to start or which ones are more important or how to make use of them. In point of fact, for all of you some of the most unhappy, difficult lives you have had, have been the most abundant. Now, you have had, perhaps, a life or two in abundance that you've enjoyed and may remember that, but if you tell me one that you have enjoyed I can give you ten that you did not.

With abundance comes responsibility. And for some of you responsibility says restrictions or limitations or my freedom is being taken away from me. So go forward in a step-by-step manner through a free flow which the universe gave you as soon as you said, "Yes, I am ready — I want to look deeply, flow deeply, so that I can learn and understand." My friends, the true meaning of free flow is being willing every moment to keep flowing freely with respect to looking at self and what you have created, being willing to keep moving even if you get discouraged, even if sometimes there doesn't seem to be any flow. But there is — there is the free flow of transformation within you. This is the basic free flow that is your divine right. That is your heritage given to you by the Creator, and it is flowing abundantly through you.

Remember, free flow basically does not bring you things as an individual. It can on one level, but it is a flow of consciousness that is ever more clearly, ever more comprehensively connected into the Plan, more loving in a way that is ever more allowing, ever more able to be aware of its divine connection.

14

Personality Bridging

You have been told over and over by your spiritual teachers to let go of the ego, to release it and center your consciousness within the higher self or the soul.

I think it is important to look at that ego, which is the center of the personality level, and see it as a bridge to a clearer life. Now, the ego has a reputation, perhaps, as the "bad guy." In my opinion this is not true. Certainly the ego-centered personality level needs to understand that it is not the center of the universe, that it is not the most important thing in the universe. It needs to see beyond its own perspective to understand its Source relationship and to see that its strengths have been developed to bridge a process for Source Itself. In the Source's individualization process, as I have discussed in a number of chapters in this material, the Source decided It wanted to learn and grow and evolve, and thus It created a multiplicity of consciousness, each piece of which is evolving.

This is a complexity and yet, in my opinion, a unique simplicity upon which evolution exists. Your ego-personality level is a center of consciousness for the Source. It is a specific that has been created for you now in this life and only in this life with which to focus the unique learning and growth of this current Earth expression. Your personality/ego, then, is held together by a sense of uniqueness. It is that uniqueness that literally keeps your consciousness from fragmenting or scattering.

Over your many physical lifetimes you developed the ability to use an ego and a personality structure. When you first came to physical existence it was not easy for you to do that. You got "spacy," and it was difficult to relate to the physical level. You all had to increase the emphasis within the personality/ego center in order to make good contact with the Earth. Now, was this absolutely necessary? No, there are a few beings who have realized completely their own divine center within physical existence immediately without going into the personality-ego level completely. But about ninety-nine and nine-tenths percent of you immersed yourselves within the ego and personality level in order to have a more comprehensive understanding of physical existence and your own part within it.

You reach a point in your evolution — and a number of you are there now — where basically life is rather "easy." That doesn't mean there is no learning, and it doesn't mean that you are always comfortable emotionally here. It does mean that anything you decide to do, you do easily and well. You have a perspective which is what I call "right."

Now, if you have done something over and over and over again until you are very good at it, certainly you may enjoy that creation that you do so well. But for many of you it sets up what I would call a boredom syndrome, meaning that you've done it so many times that it seems boring to go into it again.

As you reach a maturity level physically, or as you are about to graduate from the Earth within ten to twenty lifetimes of the ascension process, you begin to bring forth through what I have termed personality bridging the perspective of the soul or the higher self, which, when anchored in the physical structure, becomes the means to create more and more unlimitedly. In other words, the personality level goes as far as it can, it has created a centering, a strong one, a creative one, but then it must let go, it must surrender. This surrendering to a creative level greater than itself, in order to become a part of that level, is what many of you are currently engaged in.

You have heard of surrender, of course, and it is a letting-go process. A letting-go of the ego-personality's belief that the only center which truly exists is itself. Now, it seems to me important to recognize that there are many ways in which you hold on to the ego-personality, even after the soul's anchoring within your physical vehicle. One way is the belief that only your means of attaining "enlightenment," if you will, works or is correct, that no one else has a path to enlightenment, that eventually all will see it as you do. The ego-personality latches on to this idea as a part of its being the center of the universe. This erroneous belief or perception must be surrendered in order that the relationship that you have to others, to humanity, and to truly all of the whole Creator level can become clearer, more receptive and, my friend, more dynamic.

Let us say that you are within a small group, and you are excited about what you are doing. There are many who come to you, and you are helping them, and you are helping yourself. And you have created a focus which you believe is the purpose of your soul. Others come, and they share, but they have their own way, and perhaps many of them appreciate what you are doing, but do not become what I would call a disciple of your methods. How do you feel about this? Are you able to see how much "richer" you are by their sharing your perspective and then going on to their own choices? Some of you can see this clearly conceptually but emotionally can't accept it. Even if you are not an emotional person, you bury some personality-level egocentric beliefs which would like you and all that you are doing to truly be the center of the universe from a personality misperception.

Gradually you are all learning to do what you call "network," and this is very, very important. Certainly I am not saying here to give up a group focus. In point of fact, group focuses are becoming more and more important, because they put together aspects of understanding and allow a wider-scoped creativity to be accomplished. But what I am saying is that the more open you become in viewing other's choices in relationship to what you and your group are doing, the more your personality bridges in this area to the consciousness where your group vehicle surrenders to the need of all humanity.

Now this, of course, is opening what I would call a "can of worms," and before I get all groups mad at me, I want to say that this opening is really a subconscious opening. This creative opening occurs through allowing compassion and trusting the process. Then you are willing to allow all of humanity to make their choices and not try to hold onto them or to create personality judgments which restrict and limit. What does it limit? Well, my friends, it limits you and your group perspective. That's truly all that it limits. What is needed is a letting go, a bridging by the personality level to see that your transformational efforts are really nothing personal, not at all. They need not be an ego perspective. But the heart energy must bridge the needs of humanity through the group consciousness and group awareness.

Now, with this we begin to teach you what New Age groups can be. They need to recognize a unique perspective, one that is evolving and growing, but so intricately and so interwoven within the human level that they become a dynamic creative igniting point of contact within humanity. One of the best examples of this is your Christ. He gave to humanity in general, yes, but he had a group, didn't he? He had a group of twelve disciples and a larger group of followers that were his core contact with humanity, beyond the multitudes that he addressed. But he was never personal in the sense that he centered on any one group as being more important in its capacity to enter a clearer relationship with the Divine. The Christ showed how to bridge from a personality perspective to the incredibly clear perspective which he embodied at the point of ascension.

Jesus Christ on the Earth showed you specifically how to anchor love, enough of it within the personality level so that an automatic bridging process occurs that allows you to accept what humanity is creating, to become a part of that, not affected adversely by it because erroneously there are beliefs that the Christ suffered. Of course, he did not. What he did is play a role, create the bridge from the smaller center, which was important in order to establish a point from which to build a bridge to the wider perspective which allows a clear evaluation through the heart energy of what existence truly is.

All of you are ever moving out from a center. You are not losing a centering. You are gaining over and over again a perspective or center that is being fit in with larger perspectives or centers which have already been created. Let us say that you have 2,000 lives planned on the Earth, and let us look at them beyond sequential time, so we will not see them flowing one from another, because they truly don't. We would have to get into a lot about alternate realities in order to understand this. But the clearest way to look at 2,000 lives on the Earth from a point of centering is to visualize a large surface of water such as a lake. And then see 2,000 pebbles entering that water at the same time at 2,000 different places in the lake. Now, as the pebbles go in, there is a corresponding vibration that goes out from each center. View, then, each pebble's effect, each center's effect, and see how the waving-out overlaps within the centers, some touching others, some really blending and merging together, so that a greater waving-out effect is created. Can you see that each center, which is that personality level established within a physical structure, becomes a strong point from which a clearer perspective can come forth through the bridge that is built to the soul level?

If you look again at that lake and the 2,000 centers and the vibration that goes forth, you would see patterns of energy rather like a spider's web, energy centers, energy merging, energy flowing. Literally a bridge of energy surrounds one's physical existence and allows one to see that, in its totality, it is truly a personality center of something larger. So if we back off, we can see again the multiplicity of centers within the whole, of which physical existence is one small part.

One keeps backing off, if you will, until a point where your conceptual abilities have reached the extent of their understanding at the moment. In my opinion, the backing-off and looking at existence ever more expansively is eternal progression, and we will always be able to do this. Once we have seen existence as a whole in any regard, we can see that as a center from which to further explore and expand. Thus a personality bridge is truly a perspective which grows strong and which is then transcended to an understanding of how that perspective fits into a much larger or greater perspective. You can use this in any area of your life whenever you feel something is well-centered and complete. Then look at that as a point of new beginning within which to expand your understanding to a whole new creative and conceptually more complete level.

15

The Negative or Shadow Side

I use this term because many of you use it. It is not a part of my vocabulary. I consider the negative or shadow side to be in the shadow because you haven't yet realized how to light it up in your understanding. Anything that you haven't understood, therefore, is shadow.

Perhaps the greatest or most comprehensive area for many is the power area. There is a chapter in this book called "Accepting One's Divine Power." I hope that you will read it.

The negative side of yourself consists of those areas that you have kept hidden. You didn't recognize your behavior in that area. For a long time in your evolution it is difficult to be objective about yourself. It is difficult to see yourself as others see you. They are looking at all of you. They may not be consciously aware that they are, but they are. You are looking at the areas in self that you have lit up. You are not allowing yourself to look at the shadow side which is not lit up, what you consider the negative side of self.

An example of this for many of you is the heart area. You certainly know when you feel love, don't you? Well, sometimes you do. You do not yet recognize all of love's various ways of expressing. Thus you may aid others without seeing that as an expression of love. You may even say to your friends, "I don't understand love, I don't have it. I want it, but I don't even know what it is." You may have, just that day, called a friend because you knew that friend was having a hard time, or you may have written to someone and said, "This is just a note to communicate with you and let you know I care." These are expressions of love.

Now you may say to me, "I don't ever do that. I don't call anybody and I don't write, I simply live my life, and it seems to me that there is not much love in it." I would say that if you are reading this material you are more open in the love area than you know, and it is important for you to recognize that the love center is the key to resolve what you call the negative or the shadow side.

Now, there are horror movies, thrillers they call them, which show people being brutally murdered and all other kinds of violence. Participation in this could be called living in the shadow, where one is so out of balance that he has no regard for life.

However, the shadow side is in operation even more gravely in other forms of activity besides murder on the physical plane. Over the eons as you lived your physical lives you felt the ultimate threat was loss of the physical body. That certainly is not the ultimate threat, but in the mass consciousness it has been seen that way, and your movies portray it that way.

Many times there is a deeper violation or shadow effect being created in everyday life through interactions that violate ethics, that misuse power, that deliberately take away divine rights.

WHAT ARE YOUR DIVINE RIGHTS?

You have a right to be a part of the whole and to ever expand your understanding of how you fit into the whole.

You have a right to create fully and clearly in your own unique manner as you learn to do so.

You have a right to enjoy life.

You have a right to communicate with others and assist them when asked.

You do not have the right to others' creative space, to seek to force or manipulate them or to destroy their creativity on any level.

There have been those who took away others' creative space beyond the physical, and this is a much more serious violation or negative effect, and you can be sure that it is paid for by the one that commits this crime. Thus Hitler's crime against the Jews was much greater than an assassin's bullet. Hitler's motive was to entirely wipe out a whole race of beings. He had no right to seek to achieve this goal. It was a misalignment of divine power. A taking of the Creator's prerogative into the cocreator level distorts the clear use of the divine power.

All of us eventually will be the full Creator. We are not yet capable of making clear enough decisions to be that Creator. We need the support of the cocreator level, of humanity. We do not have the right to assume that we are clear enough to make decisions that usurp others' divine space and divine creative opportunities. The universe is quite severe with those who try, because it violates the process. Truly the most important relationship you have is with the Creator and this process.

16

The Friends Syndrome

I call this chapter "The Friends Syndrome." Why do I call this a syndrome? It is because friends are sometimes considered a particular group that have to be catered to, that have a control over you that you can't move beyond. Many feel that they must stay at a level where they are approved, welcomed and nurtured by their friends. If they evolve and move beyond the place of reality of their friends, they feel that they will be censured, that their connection will be lost, that communication will be withdrawn and they will lose what they have perhaps held very dear.

Now this can be true, all of it can be true, but you will, of course, make a connection to others, there will be other friendships, other bonds. And when they can be on more levels, then, indeed they are that much more pleasant, comfortable and exciting. At every level the peer group is very important to a person, and there is a deep feeling of camaraderie among friends, whether you see only one friend at a time or a group of friends. Some of you have a lot of group programming and don't enter into a group of anything, but that's taken up in another chapter. In this friendship, this kinship, it is important to see that everyone is not moving at the same pace, in the same direction or has the same purpose. Now, we feel that evolution and doing your part in the Plan is the only game in town, and I indeed agree with that. However, many, many orthodox people in various established religions are becoming lighter and lighter. Many are already lightworkers, many are allowing, many are capable of unconditional love, and because they see the world from a different concept, a different point of view, it does not make them alien or separated from you, unless, of course, they see it that way. There is no need for any one of the lightworkers to see it that way.

Now, I say to you, of course, that if you do not have the programming that says your beliefs will alienate your friends, then you will not pull it in. But if you do, then you will, because there is in the mass consciousness a great deal of programming that is different from the philosophy of creating your own life and therefore changing it when you desire, of being part of the Creator and part of the Plan. These concepts are not readily accepted in the world. They do not fit in with all of the great religions, the major religions. There is a growing New Age point of view like Unity, Religious Science, Christian Science and others that embrace some or part of this point of view, but it is still looked upon as very different and rather alien by many of those in orthodox religions. Now it depends upon their heart opening and development whether or not they consider this "evil." If they do not, then a happy and pleasant coexistence can exist between you and them.

If they do, then you can bless them and let them go, because the contacts and connections that you have through these New Age beliefs, through your channel, through your friendship with those who do believe in this way, can be more encompassing and valuable and loving, perhaps, than the former ones. You are moving too fast to be comfortable with them; however, there may be many areas that you can still find to enjoy together as long as the basic philosophical point of view does not irritate them or you. It does not throw a barrier up between you.

Do not be afraid that you will be alone and lonely because you have moved to a different level, into a different circle, because you are beginning to make your connections with those on the higher levels of existence, with some of the higher astral beings and with many of the spiritual teachers. This is indeed a comforting, warm and beautiful relationship. On the other hand, allow yourself what connections you can with humanity and recognize their shortcomings and programming with compassion and unconditional love. Help them if you can, supporting them, if they allow, in seeing what they are creating, with the interesting and exciting realization that there is such a great opening all the way to the galactic center. Friendship is a very beautiful and important thing, but are we not all friends, all part of humanity? This love relationship extends to all; there is no one that you can't learn from. You may feel not interested in what they are interested in, what they are doing, but if you look symbolically at it you will see indeed that there is a lot of interest, even if they are focused into gambling or horse racing, bowling, horseshoe throwing, eating, or hiking. Any of these activities afford considerable material on all levels to interest your evolving being. To be with someone for a period of time who has a very different interest is useful and important. Your mental body enjoys it, and it is important to allow the mental body to have some new points of view, some new, shall we say, food to digest, some new concepts to put together, new perceptions to integrate.

So allow yourself to expand your interests as much as possible; be interested in everything that humanity does, because they are all your brothers and sisters and children and parents. They are all playing out the same play, using a different cast of characters, and when you can see how all of these plays fit into the whole, then indeed you are moving toward the cocreator level. So do not avoid a contact with humanity. Everyone can be a friend, everyone can give you love; you can give everyone love, everyone has something to teach you and you to teach them, even though it may not be through verbal communication but through heart understanding, emotional enjoyment together, mental connections or the spiritual. Allow it all to happen, allow yourself to flow with everyone. Do not put up barriers — there are no aliens in humanity, nor in the animal or mineral kingdom either. We are all one, and, of course, the Hierarchy and the teachers understand that, and we love you all and consider each of you precious and interesting, and we rejoice in your development, no matter in what direction it takes you or how fast or slow it appears to be.

Remember that we are always your friends and you always have us at your call.

17

The Support of Humanity

There is a support that many do not recognize: it is the support of humanity, and whether or not you have group programming or feel that humanity is just the mass consciousness and therefore not supportive, humanity is truly supporting you. No one is an island and no one exists by themselves. You may shut yourself in your room, not communicate with others, but you will still need the room —which was built by others —and you'll need the food which is grown, prepared and served or processed by others, you will need the radio, television, lights, utilities that are all put together and serviced by others. So you cannot escape from the support of humanity. You can only escape from communicating with them about that support, and not for too long. Humanity is one great being, humanity is one woven fabric, and the sooner that you recognize your part as a thread in this fabric, the sooner you fit with happiness into your environment and can enjoy the privilege of this process. There is, then, a total beingness that is humanity, and each one has its part within it and is working to support this humanity level of operation.

Now, it is different in different parts of the world and, of course, different on different planets. Let's talk about this planet. Humanity is the intermediary between the Earth and other kingdoms, and humanity serves as a transmitter for the higher energies, the energies of the Hierarchy, to come forth to the Earth, and it serves to allow the crystals and the plants and the animals to bring forth their contributions to the planet with greater effectiveness. There are more than a thousand ways to support humanity and for humanity to give support. It is a source of happiness and contentment for those within humanity to give support to others in humanity and to give the support of humanity to the Earth.

As the Earth takes its fourth-dimensional initiation, the support of humanity is critical, and the support can only be manifested through humanity as they recognize their power. I shouldn't say it can only be manifested through them when they recognize it, because it is manifested, though the recognition is only at the subconscious level, but when this recognition reaches the conscious level, then indeed the light can be conducted to the Earth, all of the light energy; and humanity support can bolster this influx of energy at this time. You know, it takes quite a bit more energy to move than it does to stand still, and what is happening now is that the Earth is moving, and you are moving. Every day you are moving and changing, and life is moving and changing rapidly, and so a great deal more energy is required. And that energy, my friends, is there, it is there for you to invoke, it is there for you to allow, it is there for you to share in cooperation with your fellow human beings to make it an efficient and supportive energy for all you, the Earth and the Hierarchy and the other kingdoms.

Know, then, that as you work consciously with humanity toward the bringing in of the New Age and toward your own evolution and that of the rest of humanity, then you have the support of the rest of humanity. That support is there, whether you call it getting a job, playing the stock market, inheriting money, whatever it is that brings you abundance, is supported by humanity and, of course, the Source. The Source's support is always there, and it is from that that humanity gains its strength through the soul star – the energy comes and can always be increased. So look at what some of your feelings are about humanity. Do you love them and interact with them and appreciate that constant support you are receiving? Or do you not trust humanity? Do you get into conflicts every time you have a car fixed or get on a bus or work with your fellow employees or drive? Is there a feeling that all of humanity is out to get you? This is not projected if you put out unconditional love to all of humanity that you meet. Then your reward, your return flow will be love, even though there are many that you have put it out to that are not capable of love. Still you will be supported by those who are, and those whom you have grown to love will aid in supporting you as much as they can. That is your destiny. You cannot avoid being supported by humanity or supporting humanity – you can just avoid these direct contacts that you aren't comfortable with, or you can prolong the illusion that you are going it alone. That, of course, is an illusion.

The goal, of course, is to be allowing of everyone, of humanity, allowing them to have their experience - not judging that experience except when it is necessary to interact in an official capacity. Seeing how all of the experiences fit together and, therefore, what kind of mass consciousness is held and then aiding humanity to let that go — let the mass consciousness, nonproductive programming go — so that the experience of living on this Earth will be more joyous for all of humanity. Join in the joy — lead the joy — show humanity how to live as a soul upon the Earth, how to walk as a soul, how to love as a soul, how to work as a soul, how to spread the light, and lead others into the New Age.

18

Unworthiness and Insecurity

One of the prevalent resistances in those who seek spiritual advancement is unworthiness. This holds back, and has held back for a long time, many who are almost ready to ascend.

Many in humanity have the erroneous belief about physical existence which says, "I was rejected by the Father, the Creator, and sent here to this less-than-desirable place for punishment, and now I must prove to the Father that I am worthy to return." This type of scenario is repeated in many ways on many levels of the mass consciousness programming.

This confusion of unworthiness is repeated in many church services that brand humanity as unworthy of the Father's love unless their guilt is somehow expiated.

The birth process of coming forth into the active state has had that effect on many sparks of humanity, on many beings as they left that warm, cozy, knowledgeable, comfortable, safe, secure and perhaps dreamy state of support within the Creator, where they had meditated, contemplated and integrated during the cosmic night. In this birth process it was rather jarring to move into this unknown, seemingly exposed or uncomfortable, situation.

It is similar to the birth of a child as it comes from this comfortable, floating, supported environment into a cold, bright, noisy environment, where it is left alone and can no longer feel the connection with the mother. It feels unsupported.

The deepest aspect of unworthiness comes through some erroneous belief that you have failed the Creator and have therefore been rejected by Him. Failing the Creator seems to be the ultimate failure, the greatest "sin," and it is accompanied by a great deal of guilt, as unworthiness often is. There is a deep belief that you have done something unforgivable, and someone somewhere knows about it; or in some cases the belief is that everyone really knows how unworthy you are, even though you do your best to hide it.

Unworthiness is also very strong in those who are coming back from many experiences on the dark side, ones who have been only interested in their own power and have used humanity for that purpose. As they come back, there is a very deep sense of unworthiness, separation, emptiness and loneliness, because they feel unworthy of human trust and support, and they recognize an inability to love and to connect with the Divine.

To a great extent the unworthiness, then, is suffered by those who cannot accept love or their divine connection, so there is frequently a lot of alienation and separation programming and a lack of a communicative link with humanity and the Source.

There is usually difficulty in opening the heart center to

accept love, but for many there seems to be a demand by others that you give them love and caring and support. These are the ones who can never give enough. They give and give and never get anything in return because of their "unworthiness." In fact, many pull in betrayal in return, because they cannot accept that return flow of love.

This resistance that stems from unworthiness is often a large factor in the area of abundance. Many consider themselves unworthy of having abundance. They must continually prove to the Father, humanity, etc., that they deserve it.

Some feel that they deserve enough food and a place to live, but they can't have anything extra, some of the more desirable luxuries such as travel, entertainment, etc. There are many that feel that, if they have abundance, they cannot be spiritual. They prove their spirituality by having a bare minimum of existence. Some have taken the vow of poverty in many lives.

The area of insecurity is not so much abundance programming as a deep belief that you never know enough to make you qualified to teach others, to make you important enough to be recognized, or good enough to be validated, listened to, taken seriously, respected, or to be a leader in an area. These are the ones who are always supporting but never leading, who don't take credit for their excellent work. They are never even credited or acknowledged, because they project this insecurity or unworthiness. There is a feeling of betrayal and resentment that results from this.

Insecurity is based in the soul area. It is not so much an emotional body problem as a soul and mental body problem. Often there is a soul aspect that doesn't think it is capable, doesn't want to join in, is upset about the purposes chosen, and is very uncomfortable and insecure about them. This resistance, as it keeps coming up from that level, causes it to spill over into all the bodies.

It is important to look at what you are expressing. What are you not doing that you would like to do and truly have the ability to do? This may be due to a resistance in the soul or a push-pull in the choice area. There could be a strong desire to serve the Cosmic Plan in a specific way but also a deep feeling that you are pulled in another direction, and that direction is more important.

This is one of the most important and deep areas for many people, and once they have found and removed this resistance, there is usually a rapid rise to a new evolutionary level.

Look also at what you are doing and not receiving credit for, and what you feel would happen if you did receive credit or were acknowledged for it. Sometimes there is a responsibility or visibility problem perceived if you go ahead and do it. That is another area that can enter into this, and it is taken up in other chapters.

19

Parent-Child Relationships

You may not recognize that your parents' lives are reflecting beliefs that you have buried, not acknowledged, not seen, as a part of what you really believe in your relationship with the Source. Now this is not a negative statement. Those wonderful moments that you've all had with your parents also reflect the wonderful beliefs that you have in regard to the Source. It is then a synchronistic expression of the parents which shows you step by step how to sort out your Source relationship. Many of you may have parents who have difficulty accepting the new perspective or the changes in your life. They reflect an older generation's inability to move as quickly into change. Perhaps you wonder what this is mirroring to you. It is mirroring that there is not a slowing down of the acceptance process through experience. By this I mean, that when you were allowed to begin a new perspective, whether it is the Source level or in your physical life, you had a guidance system. Your parents were that guidance system. They made an agreement saying, "I'll bring this being to the Earth, into physical existence, and I will guide him/her until they are fully established on that new level."

This is a very important point but one that most of you have missed because it says to you, "When I reach a point of divine maturity that is comfortable and familiar, I must hold onto or cling to that point; because I've finally grasped that level, I mustn't let go of it or I will have nothing." Thus many times your parents reflect to you the inability to accept change. You see the example of the Source, always inspiring you and you remember the Source as It was, not as It is, and that's interesting. The Source is not in sequential time, but Its focus or Its expression is. You remember the undifferentiated Source that you originated from: that point is encoded on your memory banks. You do not recognize the Source as It is now for you because It is evolving through you. You haven't seen that completely enough yet. You are holding onto the Source as It was in your memory. Step by step you are letting go of the need to have It as It was, step by step you are accepting It as It truly is, as a changing,, growing, overall system that you are plugged into and evolving from and through. What I'm trying to say is that you are growing from the Source and It is growing from you.

Emotionally you are connected with your parents. There may be anger, there may be loss, there may be frustration, but there is also, if you get down deep enough, love and gratitude and appreciation.

You may not always recognize it, but it is there. Now with the heavenly Father or the Source it is the other way around. You recognize the love and the gratitude and bury the anger and the frustration etc. Both are a part of the same thing — your Source-level relationship. What I am saying is, look realistically at your relationship with your parents — not as you remember it especially from before, but as you view it now, because the nowness of that expression will show you the most important part of that relationship that you are learning about now.

Yes, it is important to recognize and realize what it was like when you were born and what the characteristics of your parents' lives are, but even more importantly look at that relationship now. Now, you may say to me, "My parents are dead." I tell you, "You still have a relationship with your parents. Look at what you believe about those parents, whether or not they are still on the Earth plane." Certainly it may be easier if they are still alive on the Earth, but if they are not, then attune to how you feel about a mother and how you feel about a father now and see what that is mirroring to you. You could personify them again or imagine they were here and what would they say to you if they were. So if they are not on the physical level, bring them back again as a personification and see what that relationship is, imagine it. If they are still on the Earth, look at the choices that they have made, look at what is most important in their learning right now and then see what that is mirroring to you. It may help you a great deal to look at some of your deepest fears or your anger or whatever it is, because it's being mirrored to you by a Source-level connection — your parents.

This parent relationship, then, is extremely important. Now, the traditional psychologists and psychiatrists know how important that relationship is, and the only difference between my approach and theirs is that I recognize that it is a reflection of a higher level, so if you've had counseling, look even deeper at what you learned about your relationship with your parents and you will truly see much more clearly what your relationship is with the dynamic and receptive energies of the Source Itself.

20

Communication Blocks

Communication is vital, it is essential to evolution. It is literally the flow between the aspects of Source which allows It to evolve. Being blocked here means that you have not yet allowed yourself to receive the benefits of another's perspective, which, when blended with your perspective, becomes greater.

Communication connects into the understanding you are seeking, but sometimes one cuts off that flow of communication due to some emotion which shuts down the system. That emotion may be overwhelm, it may be fear, it may be loss, it may be anger, frustration or shock. A particular emotion, then, seems to disconnect you from the flow or from communicating. I say "seems" because, of course, it truly is not possible to disconnect, but one can consciously turn off the conscious participation in the flow. You recognize and realize that you are being literally bombarded all of the time with life force. You are surrounded, immersed within life force. You can't turn off that flow – that communication – but you may not always recognize it. You may not always know what to do with it and you may not be able to use it in an integrated manner. In other words what flows communicatively must be integrated into one's understanding before it becomes a point of connection into one's evolution.

Now, if you have some heavy patterning or programming in a particular area, when through communication you come into that area, you literally do not hear what is said. Certainly you "hear it," but you are unable to make use of what is being said because it does not integrate into your understanding. What happens is this. We will use the area of love. Let us say that you have just broken up with a polarity partner and you are feeling a great deal of loss, you are sad, you are crying and emotionally you are distraught from this loss. Someone comes to you, puts their arms around you, and says, "Oh, well, you'll find someone else, someone just as good, there will be someone else who will love you and who you will love." Do you "hear" them? Well, on one level you do, but you are not able to pull yourself out of that loss, generally speaking, because there is an inability to really recognize and thus utilize this clearer point of view. Usually it is the emotional body that gets stuck or caught in a perspective and is unable to move beyond it.

Now, there is hope, of course: it lies in the releasing of that particular emotion which, in our example, is probably loss. At least perhaps you can release enough of it that you open the door to communication, so that you can hear either someone else or your own mental and spiritual perspectives telling you that you have not truly lost anything but have let go of a certain perspective enough so that you can now understand it more fully. Now, I am not saying that you must get out of a relationship before you can understand it, but perhaps in every relationship you have to let go of one perspective of its communication and your effect from it in order to allow in a clearer perspective. So there is always the need to release, the need to let go and to make what one might call a fresh start within relationships.

Now, in your life, communication is absolutely essential. As you may remember or have heard, there have been experiments done where babies were deprived of all means to communicate, and they literally wither away, they do not respond to life, because life is communication. That does not mean you have to be surrounded by a lot of people all of the time, but it does mean that you are seeking to be comfortable as communication is more consciously a part of your life. Part of everyone's programming in the area of groups is literally the communication block – feeling that you get so much communication through a group that you can't assimilate it, or perhaps, and this is a very prevalent belief, that communication through a group is never clear enough to assimilate – there are too many points of view that never agree.

Actually a group consensus or agreement is composed of a diversity of opinions that come together, and thus it creates a sense of order out of a particular situation. It does not mean that each member gives up or does not have a point of view, because that is absolutely essential to forming a group consensus. If you simply let go of your perspective in a wishy-washy way because the group has sought to come to a conclusion that is not perhaps your point of view, then you bury emotional responses which get in the way of truly accepting that group decision. You come into that agreement grudgingly. There is judgment in regard to the group's decision and this blocks the flow of communication between you and the group. You are literally setting yourself up for a loss and a less than successful association with that group. Truly, consensus and coming to a group decision is a matter of understanding that there is a creative flow and that on your path you have a unique perspective, which, as long as you are on the Earth, is going to be valid as far as your Earth journey is concerned, but that it can be guided or take place within that group consensus, that group decisions do not either force you, pressurize you or separate you in regard to the unique creative venture you are currently experiencing on the Earth.

Now we could look at it just a little bit differently beyond the Earth, but I think for this chapter the Earth experience is what I wish to emphasize. Now, groups are the New Age, and to participate fully within a group expression is a goal that all of you, literally all of you, are seeking. You may not recognize that and you may say to me, "I am not seeking that." And I will say to you, "Not yet." Your soul is not an individual, repeat, your soul is not an individual — it is part of a group expression that has an aspect of that group expression to express, but is not individual in that expression. It is unique within the group but not individual. Now, you may say that is a fine line, but, in my opinion, the difference between unique and individual is the difference between being a part of something and feeling you have the full responsibility to do it all yourself. You see, the individual applies pressure; it says, "I must do this, I am completely responsible for it, I can't really do it in association with anyone else."

Now, some of you in the purpose area are trying to teach or to aid others without taking into consideration the needs of the group. In this case the group is humanity. You, through your communication, know that humanity needs help, and you want to help them. That is your goal, but there are many of you that do not yet have the specific understanding of how to help them. The reason is that because you haven't listened to the group expression, you haven't heard through that group focus what you can do. There is not a need to duplicate over and over again efforts which are simply a supportive base for aiding humanity and which already exist within a group focus. This is a waste of effort. Now, is it then wasted by the Source Itself? Of course not, but I am talking here about the human level, and to set up a support system for aiding humanity over and over again on an individual basis detracts, distracts or blocks the full communication that is possible now on the Earth. Now, you might look at it this way: there is a law of diminishing returns; some of you may recognize that statement. You put so much effort into something, and after a certain point there really isn't any use, or it isn't practical to put any more effort into it, because you are getting less and less back. This is my point in talking about communication through a group expression. Setting up ten thousand groups to support the transformational process is infinitely more effective than setting up ten million individual perspectives which overlap and even sometimes distract or distort the more comprehensive ten-thousand-group expression.

You see, in communication we who are evolving through the system are leading ourselves ever more into a center, a clearer perspective, the ultimate group expression. We are seeking to "zero in" on that group called the cocreator level. By being willing to participate with others, to communicate within a group expression, there is a gradual, gentle blending which does not overwhelm emotionally but allows a gradual sense of the full creative freedom and expression of the cocreator level. Now, I can really hear your response to that one! "What in the world do you mean? When I get within a group I certainly don't have any freedom, when I am within a group there is never a consensus, when I am within a group, et cetera, et cetera." But do you not see that the purpose of the group is to communicate and work out the old patterns of behavior? When you are free of the communicative blocks, you will see that truly the key to group expression is communication, being willing to talk with whomever is within the group in whatever method has been set up for such communication. Use group meetings, or certain people designated as spokespersons for the group, whatever choice has been made at that time for communication, as the way to keep talking.

Now, your emotional body needs to be willing to listen, and thus it seems to me one of the most important things to clear is the area of communication and your emotional ability to listen to what is being communicated. It seems to me vital to consciously receive communication, whatever it is, no matter if you agree with it or not, but do not simply force an acceptance on your emotional body in order to comply with a group consensus. It may be your spiritual body that is forcing it on your emotional body, or a polarity partner forcing you into some sort of an agreement, or it may be within a larger group expression. If you simply feel martyred, victimized, pressured into a consensus, you then bury it emotionally. But it cannot remain buried, and you build up a group resentment that must eventually come out, sometimes explosively and sometimes so forcefully that the group literally falls apart on the physical level. You cannot, of course, separate from the ultimate group that is the cocreator level.

Recognize, then, that communication is the key to all types of clearing processes. Look deeply. Allow your emotional body to be communicated with in your processing, give it its day. Allow it to express what it is feeling, even if what you get are these deep, deep resentments and angers and fears and loss. These are your communicative blocks, and by digging around in them, by acknowledging them, by giving your emotional body a chance to "speak" through its feeling nature and release those feelings, you begin to allow a clearer group expression in a way that probably has never been possible before.

21

A Clear Physical Body

You have a physical body, and it represents literally a universal level of learning. It is a universe, then, which can show you how well you understand creating. Your soul brings to the physical level part of itself and "lays in" a blueprint. This blueprint, energized by the soul, then seeks to build its own structure on the physical level while still in the mother. However, your own beliefs that you have formed while using many, many, many physical structures affect the process. As I said, your physical structure really represents the universal level of creating. No tool could be more helpful for understanding the creative process. The Source, the Plan, has given us, has given you, a way of understanding everything through gaining an understanding of your physical body.

I would like to list certain areas which may be helpful as you seek to understand your physical structure. All of these points connect with other points of your physical structure, and you may need to study several points in order to see the universality of what your physical structure is seeking to teach you.

1. Polarity Balance – The left side of your body represents the receptive energy or the female aspect, the right side the dynamic or male aspect.

2. Head – The head represents the Plan, the Divine Plan you are building, or let's say is being built through you.

3. Neck – The neck is the connection which brings the Plan into manifestation.

4. Trunk – The trunk represents manifestation.

5. Legs & Arms – Your legs and arms represent the movement of the manifested Plan.

6. Feet – Your feet represent your understanding of the Plan and of life itself, also your foundation in accepting the unlimited manifestation of the Plan.

7. Joints – The joints in your body represent flexible movement, allowing flexibility in the movement of your evolution.

8. The Senses – The eyes, ears, touch, smell and taste all represent divine acceptance of who you are from a particular aspect. You are willing to see yourself facing the next step for you, facing what you have created. You are willing to hear opportunities coming into you. You can physically sense and feel existence as a manifestation of opportunities for you. Taste generally has to do with placing strength and ability within you in order that they may be assimilated into your life. Smell is usually allowing strength to approach you. The aroma of the strength attracts you to use it, and then you "put it on," you wear it, and then it is assimilated into you. This is symbolic, of course.

9. The Electrical Flow — Within the physical structure, represents the flow of the soul and its electrical magnetic energy. The more electrical properties you allow in the physical structure the more the soul will be there to guide your life and to create your soul's purpose on the Earth.

10. Skin — The skin represents several things. When it seems bloody or has eruptions or there are some sores on the skin, many times a deep area is surfacing, is being released, is becoming visible, and you are almost through this resistive area. This, of course, is a generalization and there may be variations in it. The skin is also a point of sensitivity which holds everything else together. It therefore may become a symbol of having a cohesive and integrative structure in the divine sense. Be able to allow yourself to receive that integration, to put it together.

11. Blood — The blood within your physical structure represents a flow system on the physical level. It also represents the evolutionary process as the soul, with its blueprinting system, is accepted in an ever-clearer manner. In other words, as you release various old patterns of behavior, the blood represents the flow of your evolution. In that step-by-step manner you seek to allow that flow to contain the elementary, the basic elements of existence which could be called physical building blocks in a manner which will build for you in your present physical structure a sense of being permanent.

In other words, the aging process will first slow down by introduction into the physical structure certain elements which are stimulative of the endocrine system, which then produces hormonal substances, and these various substances stimulate the endocrine system and all functions of the physical body to accept a permanent but evolving structure.

Over and over again you have created physical structures on the Earth. You have literally built the aging process into the system. You must now use it again, and in a step-by-step manner release that aging process. One way to release it is to look specifically at all functions within the physical body and clear resistances that you recognize and know are present. In point of fact the aging process is a symbol of having accepted, erroneously, of course, that evolution takes place through a repeated pattern of destruction.

12. Bones — The skeletal system in the structure of your body represents the structure you use on the physical level. You need a structure which is strong and fits together well, which is supportive of the Plan, and which creates a firm basis for choices which you bring into your life and the way in which you choose to live.

13. Spine — The spinal area resistances are, in my opinion, almost always either a support area problem, particularly in the lower back area, or a structural misalignment and perhaps inflexibility in the center back. What we might call the upper-center back area is many times heart-related, a problem or a resistance in opening the qualities or in accepting the qualities of the heart. The upper back, including the shoulders and the upper arms, is mostly a structural resistance. Many times an upper back resistance comes from a sense of rapid evolution and an erroneous belief that the structure can't keep up with such a rapid evolution.

14. Endocrine System — In the endocrine system there is perhaps the deepest and most helpful symbolism for understanding the physical structure. I would like to go through it with you now in order that you may use it to help you recognize any specific resistive points.

The pineal gland often represents in its resistances a *misunderstanding* in regard to the divine connection. Many times on a basic level the connection is recognized as being there, but the understanding of what that means is not present because the mental body and its conceptual abilities are not yet being fully recognized within self. The pineal then could be called an integrator of the divine connection into the four-body system.

If the divine connection is not structurally validated within the belief system yet, the emotional body will not feel supported by the connection, even if it is recognized as present. Also the physical body will be affected generally in the heart area, although for about half of those with this resistance the block basically will be between the throat and the heart. It may be perceived as a heart blockage physically, but more precisely it is centered for fully half of humanity in the connection between the heart and the throat.

The pituitary gland is also an integrative one. Perhaps we could say that most resistances, however, are concerned with seeing how the inner or soul's purpose fits into or can be coordinated with the outer expression which is seen through the physical eyes.

Clairvoyant abilities are developed here. This is the ability to see on the inner level, and generally as this ability to see is opened, it is a doorway for bringing the beauty and divine possibilities of the inner level into the outer level. Blocks in the pituitary may, then, be difficulty in accepting beauty and harmony into the outer life or seeing the worthiness of self to be a tool of the divine, which is fully beautiful and harmonious.

The pituitary also deals directly from the soul with the fire element. Certainly there is some effect on the pineal also, although symptoms of blocks usually are in the pituitary area. One assimilates or allows the fire element to stimulate the evolution, the understanding, the dynamic qualities in life, the electrical flow and the soul's magnetic energy in relationship to the fire element. The pituitary resistances, then, need to be explored by anyone who has headaches in the front of the head, particularly between the eyes and just above the physical eyes. Many times, when such pressure or pain exists, there is a very active connection with the soul level, which is a dynamic connection. And, in point of fact, this is not so much resistance as stimulation by the soul. If, of course, it becomes extremely painful, then that is resistance. But the fact that one can feel movement in the third-eye area often indicates movement in the connection with the soul in a positive sense.

There is not much understanding of the parathyroid, and for the purposes of this book I am going to include it with the thyroid in looking at resistance. Certainly the main resistance in the thyroid and parathyroid areas are allowing your will to move to the level of the Divine Will, in other words, surrendering or assimilating your will into the divine level. It does not mean a loss occurs here. You don't lose yourself at the divine level. But there may very well be fears of destruction, loss or alienation. There may be fears of being swallowed up, being smothered, being taken over, all of these erroneous conclusions as you seek to align and move your personal will into the higher level. One of the most important resistances coming to Earth now I have talked about in some other material since the Harmonic Convergence. There has been an increase in the number and kinds of basic elements which are available as building blocks physically. On the physical level new ones are coming in — the scientists are in the process of discovering them. Your thyroid and particularly the parathyroid glands have already discovered them. They come in through your ability to grasp them physically through this sensitive point in the endocrine system.

Sometimes such a new element is considered by the body to be an "invader." Its symbolism deals with the unknown, overwhelming, invading, pressurized by the evolution, accepting something so powerful that one does not feel ready for it. Basically there are fear patterns of entering into some new level which will destroy or perhaps hold one prisoner, sometimes take away your freedom — freedom can be important here. Also in the thyroid and parathyroid areas, the area of choice, seeing that you have choices to make. In the basic evolutionary process your soul makes the broadest choices. But you, on the physical level, have choices about when and how to implement the purposes of the soul which have been selected or chosen. You can do it now or you can do it later. There are always alternatives and decisions to be made as to how to flow the soul's purposes. If you have an important decision to make, the parathyroid in particular may be stirred up. For everyone the throat area symbolizes surrender, and thus it is very connected with the next gland, which resides on the heart.

Your thymus gland has been inactive since puberty. But through the connection with the soul it is now waking up. It takes the process we call transformation to awaken it. This is symbolic of opening your heart to unconditional love. The higher emotions which flow through the heart stimulate the thymus gland and wake it up. We could call this a direct stimulus from the soul level. So some symbols here in resistive areas are recognizing those higher emotions, all of them, at least 25 or 30 of them. They are:

unconditional love, trust, receptivity, allowingness, harmony, joy, gratitude, appreciation, kindness, generosity, forgiveness, etc. Each one recognized within self allows the thymus gland to become more actively present in your life as a soul-connected human being, as a soul-motivated human being. We could look at the thymus as a regulator also, for it allows the various qualities which we just listed and which are sent out by the heart, to come back to you in a reciprocal flow. It recognizes the outflow of unconditional love and picks up from the universe unconditional love and brings it back. It thus regulates, as much as you will allow it, the reciprocal exchange of the quality which you have recognized and sent out to the universe. Blocks will be in the area of accepting these heart qualities, of using them and perhaps being overwhelmed by them, even betrayed by them. Betrayal of the qualities is perhaps the most common and relevant block in past lives. You may have thought you sent out unconditional love and what you got back was certainly a sense of betrayal of your intent. Now the truth of the matter is that the love which you sent out at that point was not yet unconditional, and it brought back to you exactly what you truly believed at that point. But consciously you thought it was unconditional, and thus the system itself may have seemed to betray you.

The heart area resistances almost always indicate deep blocks in accepting the unconditional relationship with the Source Itself. A sense of betrayal by the Source or limitation received from the Source may be present. Certainly the heart area contains almost all other areas. In this material I am just giving the most common effects which block or cause resistance.

The electrical area is again importantly a part of the heart.

Now accepting one's power is not a throat resistance, as one might think, but a heart resistance. A deep sense of insecurity or unworthiness may block the acceptance of power, or a fear of misusing the power, or a fear of having the power misused against you, or a fear that your power may be misconstrued by humanity and thus misused.

There may be a fear that the physical level can't handle the amount of power which you have, a fear that the physical level is less than it and thus the power can't exist here, a fear which says humanity is not worth your sending them the qualities of the heart; blocks in the area of accepting what I call divine equality are present. True humility is the ability to see you are equal to everyone else but not greater than anyone else in the divine sense. Ego-blocks are both a part of the heart and a part of the throat, part of the thyroid and part of the thymus.

Patience is a quality of the heart, directly associated with allowing the step-by-step recognition of one's relationship to the evolutionary process. This is a heart and a thymus area. "Validating the Plan" is a function of the thymus. The pineal or heart-pineal connection is almost always important in blockages of accepting the soul's abilities and utilizing the strength of the soul. One might think of the word "strength" as a throat or thyroid area in resistances, but the flip-side or positive side of such strength is a heart-pineal connection. The heart is such an all-encompassing area that in one way or another most resistances connect into it. The endocrine glands, in connection with the kidneys, have quite a complex symbolism. Certainly the most obvious resistance is in the area of flowing away the impurities or resistive areas, releasing what we might call "waste elements" within the flow structure. But in my opinion there is a much more important resistance in the area of stabilization. The endocrines represent stability in the life process, whatever that life may be. They represent having an adequate flow of energy even more importantly than the throat or, from a different point of view, the gonad.

The adrenal glands adjust the whole system. Resistances and accepting stability are centered here. When these glands are strong, and in many of you they are, energy resistances may seem to come from the throat area, but, I repeat, the basic energy through an instability block is in this adrenal area. The block in stability for some goes deeply into the Source relationship, sensing/believing that the system itself given by the Source isn't stable, isn't constant, and thus one is forced from the divine level to "make do" with such an imperfect system. Perfection and imperfection are blocks connecting the heart and the thymus gland also.

Emotional imbalance is a resistance in the adrenal area and a part of the stability problem, whether there is an overabundance of emotional content in one's life or a buried state which blocks the usage of the emotions. These again are a part of the stability area and are directly connected with the adrenal gland. The fact that there are two of them states that there are some symbolic differences between an adrenal block on the left side of the body, or on the right side, or on both sides. A receptive or dynamic block, or a more general block. Putting these two together may be helpful as you clear your understanding of your physical universe.

The gonad area is an indicator of the number of possible blocks. Certainly it deals with basics, basic creativity and how it fits together, basic survival and how it is allowed. Compatibility of the two polarities, the ability to communicate, in my opinion, the basic communicative area is shown here, although we may connect communication truly from certain points of view with any of the levels we have already discussed. The ability to express creatively at a level is centered here. There is always a very special connection between the thyroid and the parathyroid and the gonads. One literally is a continuation of the other in a creative sense. The result of this special connection with the gonad and the pineal, when it is understood, allows the gonad level to express the clear intent of the soul, and relationships in the life will be a joyous expression of full capability, physically, mentally, emotionally and spiritually.

So the full relationship area is basically addressed or learned about here. Certainly physical love is here and all of its beliefs. The basic body processes which seem automatic are regulated here. Now, that says something important. Because what happens when, either through surgery or through an aging process, a woman's menstrual cycle ceases? Well, in one sense, there is less of a connection of the automatic processors, but it was not meant to be that way. The clear response to the ceasing of the menstrual cycle is simply a shift of the purpose of the soul into a creative "mode" which uses the parathyroid as a regulator of the basic automatic processors.

This also is why many of you have the throat area stirred up in the process of shifting the basic functions of your body into this regulatory level, and this is a comprehensive shift for many of you. It begins at the soul-merge when the soul is anchored within the physical structure. And for all of you it takes, generally speaking, of course, quite a while for this to occur, varying within the individual. But since we began to assist you in the soul-merge a few years ago, I have not seen anyone complete that shift. It is still going on, so it's rather like being caught between the levels now. You have accepted the soul after the soul-merge, but you have not yet accepted its ability to regulate its physical structure. And if the menstrual cycle has ceased for any reason within you, there is a loss of guidance of the system which has been erroneously created. I have not discussed this before, and I feel it is time for many of you to allow the parathyroid, again through a surrender process, to govern the automatic processes of your physical structure. Certainly I could go on for a long time to discuss the physical structure, but I feel that this is complete enough to assist you in many areas.

22

Emotional Releasing

Your emotional body is the key to your evolution. Many of you have heard me say this over and over again. It cannot be emphasized too much. When you realize this point, there is an acceptance which has begun. Your emotions have been used differently from the ideal that the Plan brought to you. You haven't yet seen the full use of the emotional body. Now, some of you have buried your emotions; all of you have done this somewhat, some of you have done it extensively, until the point is sometimes reached where you don't recognize emotions. For others, you may recognize in fact the focus through the emotions rather completely but still have a tendency to bury certain emotions. Your emotions then are importantly a part of your life. Emotions literally connect.

Now, for some of you it may seem as if a difficult, or what you term negative, emotion disconnects, and in a sense it does, it overlays a clearer connection which takes away from that clearer connected perspective. But in the fullest sense emotions always connect. The positive ones connect into the unlimited perspective you are seeking, the difficult emotions connect into generally a limiting or alienated or restrictive expression. Fears and loss are the emotions that you may recognize if you view life through your emotions. If you are what we call "emotionally focused" then you have certain fears that will surface and certain losses which create crying and a sense of alienation.

Those of you that are "mentally focused" will recognize what I call a mental emotion, which is anxiety, worry, stress, anxiety — these are the mental emotions which pop out from what has been buried emotionally. Now high blood pressure and hypertension or hypotension are simply a result of burying emotions so completely that they put pressure on the physical structure as well as the emotional, mental and spiritual structures. Literally this is an explosive situation — if you pack in emotional energy tighter and tighter and tighter, it must seek to escape, one way or another. You certainly don't want that escape to be through a physical illness or an emotional collapse. There are ways to release the emotional pressures that build up so as to allow yourself to connect into your potential and to encourage your more harmonious expression.

In the work in the Foundation we have found that through studying past experiences and realizing a clearer point of view, one releases emotional stresses. This is fine and it is the ultimate, as far as I am concerned, in processing. The realization process itself is the goal.

However, because emotional responses come in on many

levels from a variety of aspects and previous beliefs, one needs to process the emotional body's perspective in addition to the more generic type of processing of all four bodies in a realization session. You, as a developing facilitator of realizations, both for yourself and for others, need to be aware that until your emotional body accepts a clearer point of view, you don't have it. You may occasionally glimpse it, but the emotions must accept that point for you to use it continuously, clearly and without building up to an explosive point which blows apart, either literally or figuratively, the creative foundation you are working from. Certainly a stroke often indicates the pressure has become unbearable within a physical structure which has literally been "dumped on" by the emotional/etheric level.

Learn to utilize several systems of release as you facilitate transformation within yourself and others. Certainly visualizations are important, where one is led by a facilitator through a series of symbols, seeking to see how one feels about those symbols, as well as make realizations in regard to them. In my opinion, emotional processing need not be confrontation; there is a difference between facing something and confronting it. I am saying, face your emotions, but confrontation generally happens when one is not feeling supported spiritually as one communicates. Therefore, emotional processing in which the person is helped to realize the spiritual framework, the divine support system, the soul's light, the Source's Plan as a support system helps the emotions be willing to surface, to come out, to release.

Depressurizing the emotional body is important, but recognize that once you begin with it you may stir up deeply buried emotional responses that you can't bury again but must deal with.

There's no going back — not without a great deal of difficulty. Once you've begun to surface emotions, the emotions recognize that surfacing can be helpful. In other words, once you've made an opening and allowed them to begin to process, you're going to need to continue the process. I've stated before that clearing methods become addictive, and we could say that once you've shown your emotional body that you care enough about it to process it, it will want to be processed often. You may not recognize that, but what you will recognize is that emotions will surface, perhaps emotions that you don't want to surface, but it's better to have them surfacing than to keep burying them.

We will continue to develop ways to process, and the emotion-releasing process is a key factor in processing or seeking to become more unlimited in your life. What it means to release emotionally, then, is to align the emotions with the transformational process, rather than remain stuck in a past experience which ties up the use of the emotional body into old patterns of behavior which contain fear, anxiety, pain, loss and all other difficult emotions. Do not fear letting your emotions out, but I would suggest that you process emotionally with the help of those who understand what they are doing and can facilitate your processing in a nice, safe, comfortable environment. Recognize, then, your emotional body as a divine partner; cherish it, nurture it, it is not the "bad guy" but a beautiful part of you that is seeking to serve and has been utilized incorrectly, or at least not as clearly as you are capable of using it.

23

The Angel Perspective

There is within you an angel perspective. The angel within you knows how to link directly with the core level of being. In my opinion angels are links or connections, they are not personified especially, although the archangels are great centers which direct a specific creative effort. They are not individuals but connecting links which facilitate the process or Source. Because the angel perspective transcends any one particular level, it is as clearly used, focused or connected on the physical plane as it is on the spiritual level.

For many of you the angels often made the difference in your lives; praying for your guardian angel has often brought you a link, a connection into a basic level where you could again recognize more fully, more completely who you were. The angelic kingdom is very flexible, thus each of you can utilize an angelic perspective, and there is one which relates to you very specifically in any and all areas of your life. If you are feeling lonely, there is an angelic perspective that can help connect you beyond that loneliness. If you are feeling angry, again the angels can help. Whatever perspective needs a connection, the angels are those links, those angelic links which can widen your horizons and help you again become aware of who you are. For all of us, evolution is a process of getting in touch with the divine in an unlimited manner. The angels link together all unlimited perspectives, and by hooking into what they represent, you can more clearly see what you represent. It is important in clearing out old patterns of behavior to look and see how clearly in the past you recognized and communicated with the angels. On the inner level they are your friends, linking you into a creative level which really awakens all of the use of your strengths and abilities. They are often there to assist, protect, align and help balance, because as a divine being you contain all qualities. These aspects, your angelic perspective, the connections you are seeking are there for you always, so that the angelic perspective is not external, it is internal, but you may view it mirroring to you from an external perspective if you wish. Thus you may see some of the angels as personified: Gabriel, Ariel, Raphael, Metatron, Tzadkiel, Sandalphon; these links to a clearer understanding reside within you as a reflection of the system and they broaden your perspective through your ability to allow a surrender to what they represent. Now, if you are going across a bridge and your friend says, "Hurry up, come along with me," and you know that when you go fast you sometimes trip, you will want to view what that friend is asking you to do. You will literally want to see what that friend is suggesting. Thus you will want to evaluate the bridging process, but when you have done so, then this enthusiastic friend, the angel perspective, can lead you comfortably into a clearer and clearer perspective.

How do you contact that angel within? Well, the same way you contact the soul within. The angelic perspective is literally what connects you with that soul or with that higher self. The purpose of this book is to show you certain areas, some of which have become convoluted. Remember when you call upon a favorite archangel or the angelic hosts you are really going within your creative flow and asking the Divine Plan to supply you more fully so that you in turn may supply it more fully. It is necessary, when communicating with the angels, to show them that you find the Plan the most important thing that exists. If you do not, you certainly will get help, but it won't be as comprehensive or as helpful in integrating yourself into your purposes.

Now, let us say that you want to know those purposes. You can't figure them out, and you ask the angels to help you. What can they do? Well, they can make a connection and through that connection an opportunity can come to you. You choose whether this particular opportunity is a part of your purposes. You do have a choice, you always do, but the choice is simply the timing of what is flowing creatively, and the angelic link can ignite in your awareness a recognition of that creative flow. Certainly asking the angels for help is important. It's like saying to the Plan, "Lift me up into the Plan, help me to use it fully. I realize I am a part of it and I want to serve it comprehensively." Now, if you're going to work with the angels, it's probably important to clear any past associations which may have complicated or convoluted the relationship. If you ask me, I will tell you whether I see any such complications. It isn't there for everyone, but about 60% or even 65% of you have some material to clear out with regard to the angelic kingdom, which is the same thing as saying you have some false beliefs or misperceptions about how to link your creative process together so that it works well for you. Your ability to connect and interrelate that connection with your understanding, and your willingness to serve in this manner, can allow a clearer and clearer, more integrated, more accepting perspective to come forth. Your life is meant to be lived fully, creatively, and the angelic hosts can help you to reach that point of creativity where you can say, "Yes — I see how it all fits together. Yes — I fully understand physical existence and why I have become a part of it now."

24

Irritation

Irritation is an evidence of suppressed anger; it is a lack of patience or lack of caring about others. It is sometimes called crossness, or petulance, occasionally called by its name of anger, but it is a deep resentment, usually an anger at the process which extends to all of creation, including humanity. Irritation is really a lack of allowingness, as is anger. This lack of allowingness comes from a lack of unconditional love, a belief in the power of the Creator but not the cocreators, in other words, a belief in one's own creational ability and putting it ahead of the cocreator ability, which blends the abilities of all humanity. It is the perennial cocreator syndrome in which someone has gotten stuck at the Creator level and failed to see the step down from the Creator to the cocreators, a level at which this Creator thrust is divided and allowed to filter through the hearts of the cocreators to produce the results that Creator desires.

In other words, everyone is a creator and they all create together, and so, when you are impatient or irritated at someone's creation, this comes from a belief that the process cannot work and does not work unless this other one is producing your vision or your way of looking at perfection. Irritation has no allowingness, it is the belief that your way is the best way and perhaps the only way, and that those that cannot or will not follow it are only gumming up the works and destroying what the Creator wishes for humanity.

Irritation is also found on the physical level, and it manifests physically, sometimes in the throat chakra, sometimes in other parts of the body, the skin, etc., but the cause is somewhat the same; it is a lack of allowing the flow or the particles into the body and accepting this new style of living, this new way of physical existence. This irritation that causes a problem with the body is produced from a stuck point in which you say, "No, I cannot allow that flow, it is going to change my life too drastically," or "I cannot allow these particles, I do not know what they are, I don't recognize them and cannot accept something new. Something new has to be dangerous, distasteful or uncontrollable." This is what is happening now with many people as they endeavor to accept the fourth-dimensional flow and the new radioactive particles. The bodies rebel, and there is impact, then, on the physical body. This can be alleviated, as I said before, by increasing unconditional love for all of humanity and an allowingness that says, "I create and you create. And your creation is as good and worthy as mine and therefore I am not irritated by your creation, but I accept that as part of the tapestry of life." This way you can all enjoy it.

There are too many who have said, "Let there be light but let that light come only into me." The light shines on all, is what I'm saying. The ability to create comes from all, the process, the universes are supported by all humanity and fired up by all humanity and designed by all of humanity from their beliefs. Now, it is true that the mass consciousness of humanity has some misperceptions and erroneous beliefs, but that does not nullify each one's right to input into this tapestry their experiences as a creator, just as you are, and you need to accommodate their experiences as well as your own.

25

Accepting One's Divine Power

A ll of you are familiar with the statement of accepting one's divine power. You have heard it over and over, and you keep striving to accept it. Many of you are accepting it, more and more. There is at this time an emphasis upon the acceptance area that is generating contact with a dynamic flow in a way that has only happened once or twice before on the Earth. In Egypt many of you accepted your divine power much more clearly than you are doing now. Egypt literally is a synchronicity of the New Age which is now beginning, a glimpse of the future. It was literally out of context with your history sequentially. Thus, see Egypt as a link to your power through understanding your lives in Egypt. It is the most helpful perspective in dealing with divine power. In Egypt there were four distinct periods. The beginning or the building phase was really very similar to the present period of sequential time from about 1875 until the year 2000. In the second phase came the opportunity to begin to utilize skills and abilities and to stabilize the use of them. In the third phase Egypt reached the heights in the use of divine power. There were spiritual breakthroughs and great abilities used. Your Earth benefited, surged ahead a great deal from this Egyptian period. The fourth phase was a letting-go or a release of the power, which perhaps was not especially helpful for you as participants or for the Earth.

The Egyptian period could be equated to climbing a mountain. First you can't see the top because you are too close to it, but you know you are climbing the mountain. You can feel the exertion and sometimes a sense of strain or pressure to do what? To achieve a connection that is powerful. Then comes the beginning of your recognition that you are achieving it, you can see and accept that connection. It begins to flow. In the third phase you stand atop the mountain, having now the ability to accept what that connection has brought to you, the cosmic flow that is available. Then for a variety of reasons you decide to go down the mountain again because you do not yet clearly understand that you may take all of what you are using at the top of the mountain down to the valley. You, in one sense, leave some of your divine power on the top of the mountain. Now that's a false premise which has affected all of you since Egypt. Another perspective that is important to recognize is that about 25% of you went through at least one ascension process in ancient Egypt or you went through many advanced initiations which took you from the Earth or allowed you to graduate. However, because you had been a part of the Earth for an extended period vibrationally, you were asked to return to assist in the next age, which is the present one. You are dealing with the results of going down from the mountain and having an emotional reaction to it, not really seeing that you may bring your full power down from the heights.

Of course, that is only an analogy, because you're not really going down anywhere but into a more extensive use of those abilities or of that divine power.

I would suggest that you either ask someone such as me about your Egyptian lives, or, if you remember them yourself, go back, perhaps with the help of a facilitator, and reexperience your divine power. This Egyptian scene, where many of you had as many as 40 or 50 lives, is a powerful connector. It helps with the worthiness area, with the security area, with the free flow area, with the electric area, with literally many, many areas. You can see, glimpse, get reacquainted with the Earth as it will be. You glimpsed it, you understood it, you saw beyond seeming barriers that now loom from a physical point of view. These barriers are not real, but humanity has placed them there. One of the most prevalent now is the barrier that says, "Radiation is destructive." This electrical intensity is not meant to be a destructive force but an opening, yes, an explosive opening into a new level of being electrically, and your physical body can accept it as such. Radioactive particles are joining physical existence now, five in number at the present time, which is March 1, 1989. There are more coming. That's why I put this in a sequential framework. Literally, the flow of divine power is being stepped up, little by little, as you open up again that door to your divine power.

Now, it is important to recognize that the Earth is assuming its power, too, because then you can see that you are in a supportive framework from which to accept your divine power. Now the reason I am calling it divine power is that there are some who had accepted power but left out the divine part of it. Now, I might add that all power is divine, basically, but the divine power that I mean comes through the heart center. You cannot accept power truly except through the heart and have it be a process that is fully connected into your own unlimitedness. You can, for a while, use power that is not heart-centered, but it is an aspect of the personal will-level that, although it contains a great deal of strength, will not ultimately lead to an unlimited expression but will ultimately lead to a complete shut-down of expression. Hitler is an excellent example of such a misuse of power. There is not a shortcut through the will aspect, although it may seem as if that is true. I have written extensively about the will in some other material, and I refer you to that.

Some of you fear dynamic energy. The dynamic energy is your divine power. Certainly the receptive area of yourself, or the feminine side, must accept it so that there is a polarity interchange as the divine power functions, but this dynamic flow which can move unlimitedly through you by accepting your divine power is not something that need be feared, resisted, or resented. This gets us into the basic awareness area, which is your relationship with the source. For most of you remember the Source's evolutionary basic flow of divine power or the dynamic force. And many of you remember that before you were "born" the evolutionary process or the dynamic flow then seemed to separate you from the power that you had as an unborn or undifferentiated spark. You had, after the birth process, to be responsible for accepting that flow or power, or divine power through yourself.

This change is a very basic one, indeed, and some of you still resent it, are still angry about it or feel lost in regard to it. So, every time you seek to accept your power, it again puts you in touch with a basic emotionally charged point and your reaction is to resist it.

26

The Child Within

Have you ever watched a child at play? Suddenly they discover something new and they are very excited about it –
there is a sense then of the wonder of a child about something new
in his/her environment. Sometimes there is a sense of impatience
if the new does not respond instantly to their understanding. But
they are fascinated with what is new. Now, if we look at that
symbolically, what we see is a part of the divine process given to us
by the Creator. And the Creator has thought of everything, my
friends. This plan is wondrous. It contains absolutely everything
that is needed to learn and grow and discover. Some of us get
comfortable in existence, and we don't like to move. There is a
sense of, "I'll just hold on to what I have. I don't want to move, I
am so comfortable here. It feels so good and beside that, I need all
of what I have now. I just flow a little."

About that time the universe brings us something new, and

the child within responds. It says, "Look at that, oh, how interesting, I must know more about it." Now for each of you there is a little different response. For some of you your mind says, "I want to learn all about this. I want to explore it conceptually, I want to understand, I want to know now." For some of you this new area intuitively seems a part of your purpose and you want to include it in that purpose. Some of you wish to explore it on the physical level, going within with the senses and touching it and moving within it physically.

For many of you an emotional exploration is important. You want your feeling nature to discover this new opportunity. There are then various combinations of the above. One might look at what we could call the desire to be fit, the fitness craze in the United States and other parts of the world. Not too long ago, it wasn't considered especially important to exercise, everyone was less active. This followed an earlier period where one had to be active, because your job kept you active many, many hours, and one walked long distances, because transportation was on foot or horseback. Then followed an easier time, and it was more sedentary. From that has come a new face, a synchronistic expression of the New Age. The opportunity to get in touch with movement came to many. Now, because for many there is not yet much awareness about the full use of the spiritual body, the movement area has been explored physically, emotionally and mentally, depending upon the individual. For those who can see clearly enough, it has been placed within a spiritual format. This, the Sedona, Arizona, area has become a popular place to visit and hike, where many of the vortices connect you physically, emotionally, mentally and spiritually.

Now, you may want to know what this has to do with the child within. The child within is ever ready to move, ever ready to learn, ever ready to look at and experience and express in a different manner. The crystallization that may be there is simply flowed over or around or through, if you will. It does not affect the movement very much anyway unless the crystallization is very deep and very broad. And this, my friend, is why the system recycles physical structures over and over again, to allow the child within to lead you to a fresh, clear look at existence. Each year that you live on the Earth has a symbolic meaning. The years one through twelve deal with the child; beyond that we get into other symbols. Every year is an important synchronicity in understanding the evolvement of consciousness.

The first year is, of course, a new beginning, a time when the child is still very much tuned in to the inner expression and is adjusting to the outer world again and beginning to glimpse opportunities. First it must recognize its environment, and it begins in a comprehensive manner to explore that new environment. The child is delighted with each new connection that it views and sees, sometimes it cries but even in the crying there is a sense of renewal, of freshness, of letting go of the old pattern that is presently still a part of its life, but is being looked at from a new perspective.

Let us say that in one life you died of a deep illness, perhaps cancer, a disease in which the death process took a while on the physical level. Of course, there truly isn't any death, only change, but the cells certainly did not renew, and they become distorted in this illness. After birth into the next life, it takes about a year for your consciousness to again explore that fresh structure, that fresh new perspective and the structure that has now been born on the Earth.

The consciousness must again connect with the ideal, not with the distortion that created the illness. Now, it depends on several things how effective this is. But the child within allows a deep letting-go of old patterns of behavior. It would be like having experienced something dramatic in one room. You can now choose another room in which to be. And although you may have deep memories of the first room and even other rooms that you have been in, as you glance around, you get acquainted with your room and discover the strength within you as you connect into it. The memory of the other room begins to fade. You don't automatically go to a certain part of the room and start to sit on a piece of furniture you remember. No, this furniture is arranged differently. These are subconscious connections because, of course, consciously, as a small child you are simply busy discovering all of what is new. But within the subconscious mind there is an exploration of the new which is realigning, reassessing, and allowing, as much as possible, the old trauma to fall away. After about a year the new pattern has been accepted, and each day the child grows in awareness of how to "master" its environment, and, of course, my friends, this is the goal – to become a master of your environment. And that simply means knowing how to use it for the Plan, for your purpose as a soul.

We could go into every year of the child, and perhaps we will later. The child within, then, to summarize, is an important key or method given to all by the Creator to enjoy a fresh point of view from which to view your creative abilities. You do not use it only at the first part of a life, but it is always available, always can be contacted. It is there within you as a means to enthusiastically explore from a fresh point of view, to understand more clearly the comprehensiveness of existence beyond any restrictions or limitations you may personally have put into the process.

27

Wonder as a Leader

Many of you envision yourself speaking to large audiences as a part of your service to humanity. And this is a vision which is symbolic of the leadership of your understanding to aid others.

Some of you understand that this is perhaps symbolic at this time. It will not probably be an actual event on the physical level in the next few months. However, all of you are leaders.

Let us look at the whole as a circle. The whole contains unlimited points of light. As these lights move you may sense a connection with certain lights through their movement, through the dynamic movements they are making. You notice the light and its radiance. In the fullest sense your leadership qualities are utilized by the Plan whenever you reach a point of understanding in any area which the Plan can use comprehensively to evolve itself.

Let us put it in another way on the physical level. You are studying with a group in a classroom situation, and many of you have difficulty in grasping the subject. One of you suddenly says, "I've got it." And this person stands up and begins to share what they understand about that subject. Soon others are also communicating, and there is a general consensus that the subject matter has suddenly become more comprehensible, more generally understood. The person that stood up and said, "I've got it," had what I call an aspect of wonder; they have understood, they have said, "Aha! I see!" And they begin a process as a leader who will help others to understand and see also.

True leadership, then, is a point of contact which radiates to others and extends consciousness. A true leader is never judgmental or argumentative about their own position, but simply presents a point of view in order that it may be explored and fit into every other point of view. Some of you have had difficult encounters with leaders who seemed to force you to accept their point of view, or to live in a certain way. Thus you have beliefs which resist authority figures or make it difficult for you to accept a leadership role also.

Now, this is a vast area, and the basic leader is the Source, the Creator. So in this subject also one must dive deeply into beliefs about the Creator and what the Plan means to you. Connected into this area, of course, is the worthiness and security issue, the visibility issue. The areas of the heart are a prime issue here. Your heart and its openness allows visibility, and, of course, leaders are always visible. There is not a control aspect to leadership, not to true leadership, but there may be control issues attached to a specific human leader or to those who surround him or her.

Leadership is sought by many because it puts them at a point where direct contact is made. All of you are looking for direct contact with the Source and support within your effort. As a leader others support you — this is the purpose of leadership. It may not be stated that way, but leaders on the human level are always looking for support. On the divine level leadership is a point of contact which evolves and creates a clearer understanding of what is being explored. And the effective leader is always aware of the importance of full communication, sharing, a caring manner, being available to others. Certainly decisions are important — a leader must be capable of making decisions which are fair and objective. The clearest decisions are those which help everyone and evolve the group perspective. There is perhaps nothing more satisfying than standing in front of a group, a large group of people, and having them respond appreciatively to what you are presenting to them. As a leader you then may contact appreciation. And this, by many, is equated to love. Certainly appreciation is part of the love aspect. But audiences on the human level are not necessarily in love with or loving toward everyone who speaks to them. However, if a leader can feel an openness, then this openness stimulates within the leader the use of the heart qualities more clearly.

Now, this may be hard to see in every case, but it really is true. Those who are actors and performers have need to be noticed, a need to be appreciated, a need to have their creativity acknowledged. Many of them are extremely creative. And through their creativity the creativity of humanity evolves. There is nothing wrong with a need to be noticed. It should, however, be balanced within the overall perspective of what part you are playing in the scheme and also of other people's needs.

Leaders are often quite insecure, and they are attempting to be secure by creating an environment which is comfortable or at least responsive to them. You have had many wonderful leaders on your planet whom you would not probably consider leaders because they were not especially visible to others. But your great scientists are leaders in the fullest sense. They wonder at creation, and through their wonder they contact the new understanding. They are leaders in being a conscious link into a clearer perspective of how existence works.

Each of you needs to explore deeply your subconscious beliefs about being a leader, being visible, being secure, being able to allow the opinions of others to be something you look at when you make decisions. You need to look at your own decision-making process, because you are a leader, if only of all aspects of yourself. The wonder as a leader can come in when you truly understand what a privilege it is to be a part of the Plan. Then you truly lead the evolutionary process by means of your own strengths, your caring nature and your conscious awareness of the evolutionary process. Truly you are a leader. The wonder of that statement can do much to make you secure that you have your divine place within the scheme of things.

28

Musical Abilities

All of you in your various lives have been "musical." All of you have explored music fully, and you may or may not recognize that in this life. Why would you not, if you've explored it fully? Well, the soul incarnates on several different streams of energy, placing within certain streams some specific strengths of its creative abilities and also penetrating deeply through its strength into an area which needs resolution. Music is often a prelude to an experience which begins in a creative level which is new, not having been explored before in physical existence.

Music and becoming proficient in it can develop into an all-encompassing experience. The great musicians who lived on the Earth have spent many hours practicing in order to "perfect" their musical expression. Now, what is it they are practicing? Are they not perfect instruments of the divine already? Yes, of course they are, but what they are practicing is the ability to use the strength of the divine on the physical level. Becoming proficient in music, then, takes an almost total dedication to the chosen means of expression. This creates an intensity of focus which overcomes and releases many previous blocks which seemed resistive to being released before.

Let me give you an example. Let us say that you are born into a rather wealthy family, and at the age of eight it is recognized that you have musical abilities. Let us say your instrument is the piano, and you are given lessons, and the teacher tells you to practice your scales, to practice daily the material set up for you. Now, perhaps at the age of eight practicing may not be what you want to do, but your father and mother talk to you, and you want to please them. So you spend some time working on your music. Now the teacher says to your parents, "Your child has a great deal of ability but needs to apply him or herself." And so again they talk to you, encouraging you to practice even harder.

At this point a decision will be made by you, and it is an important one made rather early. A series of decisions you make will decide how important a part your music will play in your life. At this time the decision is made whether or not to allow music to be one area of exploration in the life. If you choose to continue, then you go on with the practicing for several years. At this point another decision is made. Do you want to keep focusing more and more of your attention on your music, because you were told you have a great deal of ability?

Again the decision — and that decision requires of you what I will call self-discipline. The ability to "hang in there with your practice," even if you are alone, long hours working very hard, missing some of the ordinary fun of the life style that you could lead without your music. The heart energy is what makes the difference here. And also how much you are able to conceptualize what you want your life to be. In other words, a good balance of the head and the heart area is what allows great musicians to begin their journey to the summit of their musical potentiality.

Music, of course, is very special. No matter what kind of music it is, no matter if it is vocal or instrumental, there is a contact made through music with what I would call the center. The center represents a center of creativity. It is very satisfying to reach the center of something. And for musicians this can come when they have performed either for others or just for themselves a particularly satisfying piece of music and feel that they have done it quite well. Now, the nature of a great musician is that they always want to do better. But when they reach a creative center, there is a sense of connection through the music which transports them to what I would call the creative heights. Many use music which has already been written, playing it as written. But more and more we will be seeing in the New Age that there is an attunement to the spiritual level which can play through your musical ability.

Do you need, then, to be a professional musician? Well, not necessarily, meaning that you need not spend 25 or 30 years to play the scales to be used as an instrument, as a divine instrument. However, generally speaking, you will be the most successful in staying with your music if you have established patterns of behavior which include self-discipline and the ability to "hang in there." Many of you have not yet achieved the sense of fulfillment which comes from entering vibrationally the radiant core. This fulfillment or satisfaction is sometimes created in a musical interpretation which seems in contact with the divine. Certainly I do not intend in this material to go into all the types of music there are, but in your realization be aware that the lifetimes you spent as a musician can show you, first, the amount of self-discipline you have often had and, second, how often you have felt the connection to the creative core through music interpretation.

Music, of course, vibrates. How often have you embodied a particular vibration and allowed that to expand your understanding of who you were? I know that it is often true. Music is synchronistic interpretation of your divine beingness as it becomes ever more clearly aligned into the Plan. You have many creative choices as you play music, the means to interpret and to express emotionally through the music. For many of you deeply involved in the transformational process, having a creative outlet such as music can be the means to be more balanced within your transformation. I know that some of you are attempting to cut down on the amount of activities rather than develop more activities. But sometimes if you have allowed yourself to learn to express musically, this ability to allow the flow will spill over to other areas of your life. The musical embodiment which you contact then breaks through certain resistive areas and allows the creative flow to be entered more easily. Certainly use your own knowingness to see if this is true for you.

What I am suggesting, however, is that you begin to use some of your natural musical expression to help balance you. Use a little toning or an instrument which is available to create a vibrational contact within you which can literally loosen resistance or crystallization or produce what I would call a harmonic, which can vibrationally contact new levels of your creativity. Enter the music as a means to becoming part of it and let it evolve you. When reading this material I am giving you, why not do a little toning in between reading the chapters. It will create a movement and allow your understanding to flow more clearly and more easily.

29

Dancing through Creation

I like to think of creation as a dancing process. By creation I mean the manifestation process, the divine as it manifests on every level. The creative principle is an unlimited process, ever expansive, ever enhancing its own understanding, ever moving freely and multiplying itself. I invite you to look at the chapter called "Joining the Multiplicities of Self" and also the "Free Flow" chapter. There are many others that fit in with this chapter.

Truly, dancing, if you think about it, is the process, is the evolutionary process. A particular dance is created in order to enjoy and explore a particular basic rhythm or flow. One is not always aware of the structure of the dance. Many of your modern dances seem completely unstructured, but that is not true. That is an illusion, because they function within a basic rhythm or, one could say, they function because there is a basic beat or rhythm to which they move. This basic beat or rhythm is the foundation or the support system with which the dance is created. Creation then needs this basic beat or rhythm and the Creator has supplied it.

Now, if you think about all of the different types of dancing there are and have been in the past, you can see that they have come forth through various explorations of rhythm. This simply means that the Source is ever changing Its modus operandi, if you will, or Its rhythmic Plan.

I have talked extensively about Cosmic Days. A Cosmic Day, to reiterate, then, is an overall concept within which a complete exploration can take place creatively. This is where the multiplicity area comes in. There are so many rhythms and beats within the overall beat that it becomes rather like knowing there is a cosmic heart which is beating, and that within that cosmic heart all of humanity functions, bringing their part and its beat into that more cosmic expression. Thus there are many heart beats or rhythms expressing together and this combination of rhythms or beats is what evolves or changes the basic rhythm of the cosmic heart.

I think this is important because it means that out of one dance and through its expression comes the next. If you will think about the history of your Earth and the type of dancing that has been uniquely expressed within all civilizations, and if you were to study it comprehensively, you would see that from one dance another evolved, and from it another, and from it another. Thus we see that the exploration of one rhythm or beat brings an expression, a dance that then moves to another level and becomes literally another dance, and that dance changes the overall beat, which then creates another opportunity to again express a different dance.

One evolves out of the other. Thus the 1920s music changed into the jazz era, although they did intermingle and were part of the same thing; we could say, then, that from that came another rhythm, which one might identify as "swing," leading to the rock 'n' roll era and to the evolving beat perspective of your modern day music. This is not a dissertation on the specific types of music that evolved one out of the other, because many were simultaneously admired and still are. Once a particular rhythm or dance has been created, it is there eternally enjoyed uniquely and appreciated for its beat. A mainstream development comes from the contact with this basic beat, and the majority or the mass consciousness on the physical level utilizes a structure which has been set up in order to dance creatively.

Can you see that if you have a building which has many, many upper floors, you have a certain number of elevators? Some may take you just to a half-way point in your building. These will get a lot of the traffic. But those going to the upper levels may have certain express elevators which go through the area that the others each stop at, but move to a higher expression in order to make a specific floor contact.

Now, this may not seem to be the same thing I was discussing, but it is. Many of you in the transformational process are making a higher contact creatively than the local elevator in its step-by-step focus within the main stream or mass consciousness level. You are learning to take the express to a higher floor, if you will. Now, does this make you better than the local elevator expression? Of course not. One is a balance of the other. You have perhaps already explored each floor, and now you move to a level of expression where your creative dance is aware of the higher floors being there, and they call to you in their beat. The rhythm of the higher-floor expression begins for you an acceleration of awareness of how many levels there really are, and then through your creative dancing you can become aware of all beats as being a part of something greater, as fitting together well.

There is no judgment in regard to the mass consciousness and its step-by-step dancing. Areas to look at in clearing the dancing through creation focus are your relationship with the free flow, your allowingness of your evolution, your relationship with the conceptual area. Certainly a polarity exploration is necessary, also worthiness, security, trust and the qualities of the heart. All of these need to be understood more clearly in order to accept your unique dance, and certainly the areas of crystallization and resistance, the areas of acceptance. I would say a key to the dancing-through-creation understanding is trust. Trust that the divine within you is able to dance even if aspects of you don't yet see how that is possible.

30

Balance

All of you are seeking greater balance. But what does the word "balance" truly mean, and how does one obtain it? This is, of course, the journey and the goal, because balance truly is a point of integration where perspectives fit together so they do not interfere with one another. And so a greater whole is created, a more aware, a more conscious point. A point of balance is always more aware. It is interesting to note that balance for one person is not at all the same as balance for another. You may be someone who has buried your emotions. Perhaps your perspective has been mentally focused. A point of balance between your emotional and mental bodies is not the same as it is for someone who has viewed life mainly through feelings or emotions and is now trying to gain a point of balance with the mental-emotional perspectives.

To reach a point of balance one utilizes all of the strengths within self, sees what opposes the use of those strengths, and clears out enough of that opposition to bring the whole effort into a point of balance. In other words, suppose that you have mental strength and your emotional needs clearing. To bring the mental-emotional perspective into a point of balance you will dive deeply into emotional resistances, but your point of balance will come when the mental strength allows the expression of the emotion enough to renew your acquaintance with a balanced perspective.

I want to discuss that very thoroughly now. You approach it from one point of view, and someone else approaches it from their own unique point of view. If you have ever watched two people interpret the same dance steps, you know that each brings through dance their unique creative understanding, which is their strength. Your strengths are the part of your divine expression which you have already recognized in yourself or are about to recognize within yourself. It can be that the strengths are just surfacing, so you are simply getting glimpses of them. Truly the key to your evolution is the recognizing of your strengths. As they are recognized you can take a look at what is opposing the use of these strengths by diving deeply into the subconscious, removing enough resistance or resolving enough of this opposition so that a point of balance is obtained, which then, remember, puts you in touch with the spiraling of the overall evolutionary process. Remember, every time you resolve what I have termed a polarity split or an opposition to the use of a strength, you can enter the basic evolutionary process which the Creator has "laid in" to existence. A lot of effort is not needed in your evolution as far as "making it" flow. It is simply a process of releasing the difficult or resistive blocks. This allows the natural state of balance to be achieved, which generates the dynamic contact in your life.

All of you are seeking to understand the dynamic energy. You do not, I repeat, do not need to force an effort here to contact the dynamic energy. All you need to do is reach a point of balance in any one area and that dynamic energy ignites within you that point of balance, holding it and supporting it as the evolutionary process then takes place. Can you not see that the Creator has thought of everything within Its Plan? There is not anything which has been left to chance or random effect. Anytime, anywhere a point of balance is achieved a dynamic contact is made. Thus balance can be the key to learning and growing more aware of the dynamic content of yourself and of the universe.

31

The Polarity Split

What I mean by a polarity split are beliefs which say the polarities are always opposing factors that do not cooperate or harmonize. They are used within this polarity split area as automatically rejecting the other polarity's point of view, not able to use the polarity connection in an integrated manner, and thus taking away any possibility of allowing a sense of integration to come in through communication. I am using communication here beyond the human level. In other words, not only your communication with other human beings but within all aspects of self, within the other kingdoms — animal, plant and mineral, the overall Earth perspective, the mass consciousness and certainly the entire spiritual perspective.

Those of you that have a splitting of the polarity area literally keep moving; movement is easily obtained, but the movement is never seen as supported. There is a sense of alienation or separation brought through such a polarity split. Whether you are currently in a male or female body makes no difference as far as this splitting is concerned. The beliefs literally say that man is not supportive of woman and woman is not supportive of man, or that the receptive energies are never supported by the dynamic energies, and the dynamic energies are never supported by the receptive energies. They split off or go in opposite directions creatively. Therefore integration is always difficult because it comes through a great deal of resistance to split off or splinter creative activity into many, many parts.

Have you ever noticed a mirror when a rock smashed it and it splintered? Many segments of the mirror are fragmented. Now the fragmented mirror still functions, but this splintering does not allow a creative expansion that uses all aspects, all parts. The splintering is difficult to heal or mend without going into the polarity split area. Thus if you are told that integration is important for you, look deeply into your beliefs about polarity, as this insistence on splitting the polarity may be the basic cause of your difficulty in integration. Another way of looking at this is, if in your life you are trying to allow a wider creative base without success, if every time you begin an effort that you know is expansive, it closes down on you, and it doesn't seem possible to continue it, then look at this splintering and polarity split area. See if basically you really do not believe that the polarities can work together, can be creative together, can join their purposes together.

The basic issue is also in the area of the Source and Its evolving perspective. The basic fallacies in this splitting are beliefs which say that the Source, as It splits into individual perspectives, cannot receive in as large a capacity as before. Thus the male or dynamic energy, which represents in this case the Source's evolution, is split off from these fragmented (individual) perspectives that do not seem as able to receive. Thus the receiving literally seems to be an opposition factor in regard to the evolution or the dynamic process.

In other words, as the spiral of evolution passes through various levels of receiving, it seems to fragment each level of creativity, does not allow it to receive as completely as the Source in Its unlimited manner is able to receive.

Now you may say to me, "Well, how is that a false premise? Is each part able to receive as much as the overall part?" Well, it is able to receive unlimitedly through its own perspective, it is not meant to receive exactly the same as the perspective that has given it birth. It is never, after going through the individualization process, meant to receive as before. Because of the individualization process of evolution, it is ever locking into or clarifying its own unique perspective, which certainly is a perspective of wholeness. There is not a duplication of creative efforts ever made in the universe. It isn't meant to be that way, and yet through this polarity split scenario there are beliefs that say, "If it is not as it was or as it has been or as the Source has seen it in its overall perspective already, then it is not an integrated perspective of the whole." That is where the fallacy lies. It is an interpretation that does not see the unique points of creation as being literally the newborn Source Itself, and these new perspectives are each blending and creating that overall united perspective that we call evolution.

Let's look at it this way. A couple gets married, and they give birth to a son; a little further along they give birth to a daughter and perhaps a second son and a second daughter, so now they have four children. They soon find out that the children have a little different idea of how to create than the parents do. Now the parents seek to input to the children what they think is important in life, a sense of ethics, a sense of principles, a sense of responsibility. They give them the framework for creation and for their lives, but if they are wise parents they encourage their children's unique creative abilities through communication and through sharing with them. They encourage them to be creative in their own right.

The universe in its expansion encourages unique perspectives of creativity. That is not splitting off a creative effort, it is not saying that these children are less creative than their parents, no matter what age they are on the physical level. A ten-year-old son is as creative as the father, it simply manifests a little differently. In point of fact, because they are closer to a point of new beginning, there may be more openness to the creative area at ten than at a later age. Adults sometimes settle into patterns of behavior that resist change, particularly on the physical level.

It is important, then, to be fully supportive of everyone in their creativity, whether or not you can see them manifesting unique creativity. Who they are is uniquely creative, and when humanity begins to validate that unique creativity rather than seeking to mass produce behavior through an outmoded educational system, that will allow the creativity level of the Earth to respond to what is more natural. Now, I am not criticizing any particular educational program here, but I am saying that this polarity split of individualization from the Creator has created, first of all, a sense of frustration in regard to unification of the system. Thus anything that seems to create physical responses that are similar to one another seems to be a unification process. I do not see it that way. In point of fact, what has been missing on the Earth is encouragement of individual or unique creativity so that it, through that encouragement, begins to respond to or realize its cosmic equivalency here on the Earth.

What I am telling you is that this polarity split between humanity and the Creator is so deeply ingrained in the mass consciousness that it is reflected to you through most of the educational systems. Now, there have been certain parents and certain teachers who realized how important it is to encourage unique creativity, and there have been many that felt that they wanted to but felt restricted by the system. So an important key here in releasing the polarity-split area is to recognize and realize that there is a system that supports the full development of unique creativity, that it is possible to integrate it, that there isn't a splitting off or a splintering of the system itself through allowing support. It is interesting to note the United States in the 1960s and to see the rebellion that occurred as the system seemed to stifle and to be not what many young people wanted. They sought to force the system to allow them their creativity. Now the system expanded somewhat after that, but perhaps a clearer level of communication between those that administer the system and another generation, which literally is developing the system, is necessary.

I give you food for thought here, and now we will return it to a more personal level. If you as an individual really believe that the system is supporting your creativity, then it will, and it doesn't really matter how restricted the system seems to others or looks to everyone, you will find support for expanding your unique creativity. It may come in a way that is unusual, but it will come in, because, my friend, that is the natural state or the overall design that the Creator has given to you here on the Earth. The Earth itself is much clearer in this regard than ever before. Now it may not look like that overall, but what you begin to notice are communicative links that unite various regional systems into a more supported system overall.

As you evolve your understanding of a polarity split, seek to see if betrayal, loss, alienation, separation, sometimes anger and frustration are part of your emotional body's perspective. If you are often given affirmations by me with these words in them, then very likely you have, somewhat at least, a polarity split. Because there are, of course, degrees within it; some of you just split off in certain activities or certain perspectives, keeping a rather integrated perspective mainly. For others of you there is a more general splitting off, so that almost every activity which is thrust into your consciousness is denied the reception that it needs; it literally is thrust out again, so that what you have is the constant thrust working by itself, and the need to receive working by itself but no communication that is effective. It acts almost like a boomerang which takes you out of it again. It is important to get a clear understanding of the dynamic energies and of the receptive energies and of your precise, exact beliefs about how they interact. For many of you there are as many as twelve levels that will affect this polarity-split area. For others there is only one level or one perspective. Unification or integration of your creativity can be gained. You can springboard into it through the heart area. Certainly I refer you in this material to chapter 4, "Bridging"; chapter 7, "Support of the Soul"; chapter 11, "Unconditional Love"; chapter 13, "Free Flow"; and to chapter 19, "Parent-Child Relationships." There are many others, of course, and what I am hoping for in this material is that one understanding will bridge for you to an understanding in another area.

32

The Galactic Connection

The words "galactic connection" sometimes bring the image of something very remote to humanity, but the reason that we are introducing this now is that humanity is ready for it. Now that does not mean that everyone in humanity is ready for it, but it is the next stretch for humanity — to recognize that it has neighbors. Your neighbors are not only the planets of the solar system with which by now many are familiar. Many of the planets have been visited by your space explorers. But it is important to recognize that there is a whole galaxy out there, and there are literally thousands and thousands, in fact millions of planets that are there to be visited, to be explored, to be enjoyed, and you have touched now the beginning of this great adventure that you will be led into in the New Age. You will have several space ports on this planet, and from there you will visit these many other planets.

Star Trek and *Star Wars* are not phantoms of the imagination or dreams of the science fiction writers, but, we might say, documentaries of what will go on in space in the future. You could say these scenarios were selected from future incidents relating to your Earth and others, and there is much excitement as the cultures mix, as you confront new and unusual ways of operating, as you allow yourself to be open enough to welcome people of another color, another bodily shape, another view point, perhaps some even of no form at all. This will be part of humanity's lessons in the years to come, because the time has come for your planet to join the Federation of Planets that protects and regulates planetary travel and interplanetary relations and facilitates this meeting of your neighbors — soon to be your friends. It will be in the not-too-distant future that you will be sending ambassadors to the galactic center, where they will meet with the ambassadors from the many, many planets. Before that even, you will send an ambassador to your sector of the galaxy, for it is so large that it operates through separate organizations, separate sectors. Then later to the center, and then you will spread out in exploration, perhaps under the rules and general guidance of the Federation.

Are you ready for this? You may think that you are, and you may feel very excited anticipating this new adventure, this new aspect of life. But examine whether or not you are open enough to accept, say, a being with different skin — an alligator-type skin or a being with more than two arms or a different type of head or a tail. There are many different body models, though as I have told you before, the type of body you have, which we call the Adam Cadmon, is quite generally used in many, many of the planets and there are some variations on it, but nevertheless there are many that use very different types of physical structures, so you need to recognize the heart qualities. All of the structures have something resembling a heart, because that is the center that is connected to the spiritual level. It is through sensing the movement of the heart area that you test the intentions of those extraterrestrial or space brothers that you meet, for you will meet them walking down the street. Now you will not know them, the ones that are still of this Adam Cadmon body or able to project one. You will not recognize them as space men, but they may ask you for help and tell you that they need someone that can fill them in, make them familiar with the planet. In fact, one may be assigned to you later, and this will not come right away but later, probably 50 more years into the New Age before an actual program of exchange is set up.

If you feel, however, that you have been approached by an extraterrestrial or you are being approached by an extraterrestrial, then attune to their heart and feel – see if there is a movement there, see if there is a love coming forth. Now, many people do not have a lot of love, their hearts are rather closed off, but there is movement there anyway, and this is also true of the space brothers. If there is no movement, if there is a coldness there that seems stuck, then perhaps it is better not to pursue that acquaintance. That, of course, is the case with Earthlings who have that sort of a structure in the heart area, because it means that they have separated themselves from the light and they are operating on a personal power trip. However, most that you meet will be loving and eager to explore and make acquaintances and understand the Earth.

I hope you will make them welcome. Now, as I said, you will learn much from this connection because you will be able to ask them questions, too, of course, and you will learn about new governments that operate much differently from yours, about different terrain and how they handle it — their environment, their plant life, their animal life, the mineral life on the planets — and you will learn what their values are. And what do you think you will find? Of course infinitely more variety, but when it comes down to the, shall we say, "nitty-gritty," you will find beings who need the same things you do, who have a connection to the Creator; some of them recognize it more than others, just as on this planet. You will find ones more interested in science, music, art, just as on this planet. The very basic spiritual levels are in all of the planetary lives. Now, some of them are limited. Many planets are much more ordered and organized than Earth, and while it, of course, brings them peace, since most of them have organized in a much more peaceful manner, it does not allow for quite as much creativity. The scope of creativity is limited, though creativity in certain areas is encouraged greatly and can be developed to a large extent. You will find some very, very beautiful works of art on the other planets that you visit.

The technical/scientific and artistic information and development that you will see will move the Earth forward, practically catapult it forward into the New Age and bring experiences into your life that have been only imagined in your science fiction or fantasy, and I recommend that you allow this and not be overwhelmed by the changes and the newness that are brought in but allow it to expand you as it is meant to do at this time.

33

The Twin Souls Syndrome

There are many ways to look at everything. In point of fact, it is probably important to look at different perspectives differently. There is not just one way to look at or do anything. Twin souls to me, then, are divine perspectives which vibrate compatibly, in fact they are so compatible that they complement each other in almost every respect. They mirror or reflect to each other in such a way that each feels complete. Another way that I have defined the twin souls syndrome is that certain beings are Source-level neighbors, really being generated from the Source, not at the same time, because it is not sequential, but they've activated together. Their purposes are generally in the same spiritual area and their perspectives fit together from the divine level very well.

Generally twin souls exist for service purposes, but when one talks about them on the physical level, what the mass consciousness recognizes is polarity compatibility or the love aspect; sometimes they are called twin flames. This, of course, is important, but more basic is the stimulation of the two souls so that there is a creative unity or coming together which literally ignites or sparks to a point where the two souls function as one. They are not one. They are not halves of something – they are whole in their own right, but together they become much greater, their perspectives are multiplied at least ten times by their coming together, their unity.

Now it seems to me that some of the perspectives given on twin souls are not complete. If we look at this area on the physical level, we can agree that generally speaking there is someone on the Earth, who if you joined with them, would create a sense of completion creatively. However, in my opinion, for most of you it's not just one but perhaps three, four or even five that you could accomplish this completion with. In all of the cosmos there are probably, for all of you, two or three hundred souls with which there is that level of completion. I know it is romantic to think that there is one being for you alone that has been created as your twin flame or twin soul, but this perspective negates the universe's ability to function multipurposefully in many ways. There are many ways of accomplishing something, and it is not logical to see a twin soul as only one perspective, and that there is no other that exists. I like to think of twin souls as a mirror, and are there not many ways of mirroring? Humanity is learning to mirror clearly. Certainly the mirroring process is part of Earth living. Others mirror to you what you do not yet understand, but having a complementary mirror which brings to you the divine qualities either receptively or dynamically, in such a way that you can accept them and love them, is, in my opinion, the purpose of the twin soul.

Now, humanity hasn't always used what the Creator has given clearly. I think we all know that. Certainly you are trying to use opportunities and the Plan wisely, I'm not saying that, but you haven't yet seen or acknowledged what twin souls' purposes are. Thus what we've noticed, we being your teachers on the spiritual level, is that certain souls have said, "I'm not going to get in touch with this complementary soul because, when I do, it seems to create such an intense focus and a perspective looking only at that soul that the rest of life's learning is literally ignored." Have you ever noticed two lovers who are completely wrapped up in one another? They hardly know anyone else exists. Generally this is only part of a honeymoon, but there are those who literally are compatible enough that we would call them twin souls, but who are so wrapped up in one another that life literally passes them by. They are certainly learning about love, but it is perhaps necessary to put love in a larger framework than just with one other person in your life.

Now I am not negating or invalidating twin souls, and I think that for some of you the desire to have a relationship that is completely compatible is so important that you can inspire yourself to it through this twin soul syndrome, but it is not to be used as an excuse system to avoid contact with others or with Earth responsibilities. I am a spiritual psychiatrist, I function that way on the outer planes and certainly on the inner planes, and I feel that this whole area of twin souls will need to be explained much more clearly in the New Age. I have not talked about it much, but I do realize that those of you who have experienced a completely compatible relationship on the physical level long for it again, and also those of you who have not, long to experience it. I say to you that you can certainly have this type of relationship, and whether or not you call it a twin soul is really not important. Within the universe are many that complement you, and you can creatively build a compatible life together with these choices that you have.

34

The Twilight Zone

It is important to consider what "The Twilight Zone" means. Twilight is a time of change, when the sun is going down and its visibility becomes less available. There are times in your life when the guidance of your soul may seem less available. You struggle to understand who you are and you struggle to see that all is light. You may struggle to understand, but seemingly nothing that you can recognize brightly illuminates your particular situation at that moment. Emotionally you may feel cut off, mentally you may feel confused. Spiritually you don't feel especially connected with that spiritual perspective, and there may be pain of distress in the physical body also. Generally speaking, the twilight zone is a prelude to a great leap forward in consciousness.

You have a lamp illuminating your room well, but you realize that if you put a larger bulb in the lamp, it will give you greater light; and also perhaps repositioning the lamp will redistribute the light in the room better. So you take your lamp and you unplug it and move it to the new position in your room and plug it in there. The Twilight Zone is the period when you realize greater light is available from your lamp and you are in the process of unscrewing the old bulb and replacing it with a larger one, then unplugging your lamp and moving to a different place in the room. The Twilight Zone is always a very active and inactive period. It is active internally, but it may seem inactive externally.

Now, while in the twilight zone you may not realize all of the activities that are going on in all of the aspects of self because, remember, one of these specific beliefs about that zone is that there is less light available, and a sense of being cut off or alienated is almost always present. But by backing off a little objectively and discussing the situation with me, it can help you the next time you are readjusting both the light wattage within the cellular level as it shines upon existence, and also repositioning your new enhanced light perspective.

You might say that through such a process one adjusts or recognizes more clearly what their role is, both within humanity and within the Whole on the universal level. There are constantly adjustment periods. You are always learning or growing or realizing beyond what you now recognize, but the Twilight Zone, as I call it, is meant to indicate a point where literally all four of your bodies are encompassingly engaged in change in such a way that, even if you are clearer in each perspective of your four bodies (spiritual, mental, emotional and physical), there is a vast amount of switching electrically, and this seems to make the integrated contact or linkage between all of the bodies unavailable at this point, and this is sometimes confusing.

I think it is important to recognize that all of you have a few (three to six for most) very deep areas that you are sorting out. For 90% of you the polarity area is one of these. When you are literally going to a new comprehensive level of understanding in one of these deep areas, everything switches. You could say that you are rewired electrically. Now the electrical flow still continues in old habit patterns. Certainly it does not yet follow the divine ideal which it is capable of following within your etheric and physical structure, but through these periods of adjustment that I have called the Twilight Zone you are able to allow a clearer use of the electrical flow of the soul within you.

Thus there is a shift in emphasis electrically, and the cells begin to respond in a manner that is clearer and allows a more comprehensive use of the soul's energy. It is rather like cleaning house. When you throw out what you are really not using, then the house traffic pattern is easier; you don't have obstacles in the way. Thus in the Twilight Zone in this time of adjustment there may be some unexpected opportunities or unexpected encounters. If you remove an obstacle, then what is natural begins to flow, but remember you have blocked that so long that you may not recognize what is natural when it knocks at your door. We could say that this new opportunity, when it knocks, whether it be a person or an idea, seems alien, and there is some fear generated from this unknown contact.

It seems to take time on Earth to get through these periods of adjustment and reassess the new level of awareness that you are now in and what opportunities are a part of it. Your mental body and the spiritual, of course, are the first to be supportive of your understanding on this new level. The emotional body is busy connecting into the new level and the physical body in reinforcing its support system, which can allow it to generate the light contact or the clear creative flow that you are seeking.

Thus our Twilight Zone is really a period of adjustment on all levels when you begin to respond to a clearer call of the soul. You begin to listen at that level and allow yourself to utilize all of the resources that lie within that level of awareness.

35

Walking the Earth as a Soul

To walk the Earth as a soul is your goal. Whether you have realized it or not, your soul came to this Earth strictly for this purpose and wants to work through you on the Earth, in physical existence. Now, you may feel that the soul is not qualified for this, but indeed it knows much better than your ego/personality how to handle physical existence. The soul has the overall view of your mission, the soul knows what it wants to accomplish and how to do it. That does not mean that your choice is being taken from you in some way, for you are your soul and that is where your identity is established.

The personality/ego is a mass that you have created and put between your soul and humanity. It consists of many little behavior patterns and defense patterns and patterns that make others like you, that keep you from punishment, that advance you socially and help you to hide from yourself the truth. It also has inspirational patterns, work patterns, love patterns that sustain you as well, and this conglomeration you call a personality and the ego has worked hard to protect and develop this personality, and there is a great deal of resistance to letting it go and letting it be permeated by the soul. Actually, you do not have to let it go, you can just move it over, allow it to still use the strengths but accept the guidance from the soul level. This is really the best of both worlds, and so when your soul asks you to do something, then allow it to be visible, trust that it knows what it's doing; do not resist because of some need or desire that you are holding on to erroneously. If you let those desires go and look at the whole picture, you will find much more happiness, much more contentment.

To walk the Earth as a soul takes complete trust in that spiritual area and it has, in your perception, often failed you before. So it is to you like a leap of faith, but actually it is just a correction of your misperception. There is a welcoming of the true level to guide you, there is an acknowledgment that you are one with the one Creator and the one humanity and the one kingdom of the Earth, that you accept all of them as equally important, that you accept all of humanity as equally important, and that you continue to do your duty on the Earth as a soul.

36

Unlimited Expression

The word "unlimitedness" is one that has been used by me, Vywamus, and other spiritual teachers over and over again. You have heard it, you have sought to realize what it means. The very nature of unlimitedness means there is always a change, always a growing perspective in regard to a more unlimited perspective. Unlimitedness, then, is literally the process of evolving eternally without obscuring or distorting that growth. There are levels of unlimitedness and aspects within which one learns about it. Certainly on the physical level, let's say certainly on the physical plane, a level of realization about unlimitedness is built into the divine support system for this planet.

The Planetary Logos, Sanat Kumara, as a cosmic being, has created a divine framework with his consciousness through which each human being evolves or grows or becomes more unlimited. When you have explored this complete framework or conceptual premise which the Earth represents, you move up a level to explore again another level, another part of unlimitedness. As ascension takes place from the Earth you feel unlimited, you have made contact with the divine support system made available through the consciousness of Sanat Kumara, and as ascension takes place through this integrative perspective, you feel whole, complete, and virtually unlimited.

This is the way the Plan grows and evolves through levels, much as you realize in graduating from a school that, by allowing this learning which the school represents, you now have a tool, let's say a creative tool, which allows you to express more unlimitedly. Now, some of you in your school may not have used the process as comprehensively as it was possible to do, but all of you gained a more unlimited expression through the learning that the school represents. Learning then, leads to a new level of expression which is ever more unlimited, ever freer of limitation, restriction, distortion and alienation.

It is not always easy to assess on the physical level that one is becoming more unlimited. There are too many complexities through old patterns of behavior through ancient lives, through your association with all sorts of aspects of the Earth itself, and perhaps basically through the Sanat Kumara connection, which serves as your physical divine support system. All of these patterns dance creatively within you, seeking to be integrated, seeking to be a part of who you are. This means that those areas you have not yet understood or emotionally connected to in the present, are in there preventing you from seeing that today you are more unlimited than you were yesterday.

If this sounds complex, in order to see it more clearly, let me give you the following example. You have gone to a class in which a new dance is being taught. It's one that nobody knows, but it's rather similar to several other dances, and some people know one and some people know the other of these similar dances, but they are not quite the same. This new step, this new dance, is the one that everyone has come to learn. Let us say that the room is large, there are 2,000 couples, and they begin to dance. Now the instructors, and let's say there are many, have given the basic instruction and now they're going around and assisting the couples to dance.

Now, some of the old patterns of behavior may be in the way, and some of the old dances may be partially what some are doing rather than allowing themselves to dance the new steps. If you back off and take a look at that room, the process is difficult to assess, how much is being assimilated, how much is being learned. Look at all of that activity, but some of it surely is a dance that's been done before.

What do you mean that this is a new expression? "I can't see it clearly," is what I hear some of you saying in your lives. You are now able to see that each couple of the 2,000 is assisting the group to learn the dance, and each couple is letting go of the old perspectives of dancing gradually, and that the whole process is truly evolving and growing. We now flip, like we might with a video movie, in fast-forward to two months ahead and look at the same 2,000 couples dancing. Now they've practiced for two months, let us say twice a week. Look at the difference. There is a much clearer perspective of dancing. You can see it. The rhythm is clearer, the steps are more securely done. They have accepted the new dance, and you can see that by flipping forward sequentially. But at some point in a new beginning, when the steps are introduced, it is indeed sometimes difficult to recognize that each step that you take leads to a more unlimited expression.

Trust is needed here. Trusting what? The process. The divine process which is leading you step by step into your unlimited expression. Daily you grow. Daily you evolve, but indeed, trust must be used as you process your expression and allow unlimitedness.

The worthiness area and the security area are important here, and I refer you to that chapter. As one evolves, it is necessary to feel worthy and secure within the process in order to accept that a more unlimited expression can literally move through you. It is also important to look at the dynamic energy. See the chapter on accepting one's divine power in order to realize that a more unlimited expression is always present within you.

Truly, it is again the emotional body which must accept unlimitedness. Once it has seen that every moment is more unlimited than the past moment, the emotional body is beginning to move toward that point which we call the eternal now, where it has let go of the connections that keep it focused on what has been and will allow the eternal application of unlimitedness within which to grow and evolve.

37

Support/Structure

Support is something everyone needs and looks for. Some look for it from their family, friends, relatives, social structures, governments etc. That support is available from all of those areas, but what you really need is the support of your soul and your monad. In other words, through your identity as a soul you have the support of the heart structure that is connected always to the Source, and that is the main support that you need. You need to know that the Source is ever supportive of you and that you can count on It at all times. Now I'm not saying It is going to pull you out of your programming dilemmas. It will if you allow It, invoke it. But what It will do is give you that peace of mind, that tranquillity of spirit, that knowledge that you are not alone. That heart support affirms that you are a part of something greater, and that there is no way that that can be taken away from you, that you have a very important role in that greater plan, in that greater being, and that you are worthy of that role and worthy of being supported, and mainly that you trust the support of that structure.

When you feel unsupported by anyone whom you feel should be supporting you, look then at what way you are not accepting the support of the Creator, the support of your soul, for somewhere there is a gap or a lack of connection to that very, very basic part of self that can connect you into your Source-level support.

The support that you require when you are going about your daily life is tied up within the basic structure of the Source. This structure supports all aspects of creation, and it is specialized, so if you come from a certain part of the Source, you have special qualities that make it easier for you to partake of a certain ray or a certain interest or a certain occupation. There is, however, all potentiality within each one, but you become specialized like the cells become specialized. Now if you, for instance, change rays or move into a different field, you then, shall we say, get on a different track, and sometimes that support structure does not feel as supportive, but it is there and room can be made for you in that other area. It is a matter of a small adjustment in the blueprint of the overall cosmic structure. It is important, therefore, to know that you are supported in whatever way you choose to function, and that your piece in the cosmic pie, so to speak, is not so fixed that you are locked in. A possibility of change of venue, change of interest is always there. You have that freedom of choice, and that freedom of choice overrules any part of the basic Cosmic Plan for you, but of course it slows you up in your movement toward your evolution, because if you have to make these many adjustments to move into various categories or support systems within the Source, then you are slower at obtaining the evolutionary point that you desire. Therefore aligning with the Divine Plan, with the blueprint as it was laid out, is the most efficient, rapid and smooth, easy-flowing way to fulfill your evolution and come back to the point of the cocreator level, but there is no pressure from the Creator for you to do this. The Creator loves experience and is content that you experience as long as you desire, in any way that you desire.

Therefore allow yourself to know that the structure supports you regardless of how you decide to use it. It supports your choices and supports your experiencing without judgment. The only judgment you really experience is your own. Sometimes it seems that someone else is judging you, but if you do not accept it, then the judgment is not there for you.

So realize that in the Cosmic Plan you have an easy path back that was charted by the Creator, and you have many, many zig-zag paths that you can take, and so the longer you put off merging with your soul, aligning with the Divine Plan, using the divine blueprint or however you want to put it, then the more experiencing you will receive, and perhaps you will like that and perhaps not, but it is your choice. Some do like it, some never tire of the physical experience and are comfortable in using it over and over, and can use it well enough to be very comfortable in it, but eventually there is always something within them that says there is more that they wish to experience and other levels they wish to explore. Remember, too, that you are supported by all of the other kingdoms: the plant, animal and mineral. Especially you have been noticing the crystal support lately. Remember that the Earth provides the means of getting all of that support, and so allow that to figure into your gratefulness for this life in physical existence, and if you truly enjoy this life, then indeed sing the praises of all of the other kingdoms, for without them this would not be possible.

38

Responsibility

You are responsible for the level that is under your control and administration. This does not have to be fully manned by you, it only has to be monitored by you in a way that is responsive to what is going on. Each person needs to understand that they have the ability to make this response. Responsibility is another ability in leadership. It is the ability to be aware of what is happening and then fix it if it isn't right. There are those who have a fear of taking on a responsibility in a relationship, in a business, in a job, or almost any area that you may think of. The resistances spring from a perception of: (1) unworthiness to take on responsibility, (2) inability to take it on, (3) not desiring the burden of responsibility, (4) belief that it conflicts with freedom, (5) belief that it impedes happiness, (6) belief that it does not allow other potentialities to be developed, (7) belief that it will make you dull or stuck, (8) belief that the child in you will be suppressed, (9) belief by the emotional body that it will not be allowed to have any of the enjoyments, comfort factors or freedom it desires, (10) fear of failing, (11) fear of being trapped, (12) fear of not being allowed to ever let go of a responsibility – being within it forever, (13) fear of having to give up something more important because of it, impacting the choice area, (14) holding on to an old responsibility, (15) conflictive responsibilities, (16) guilt about failing the Creator in responsibility, (17) anger or hostility about being forced to accept responsibilities that you do not desire, for instance the responsibility of life, of being an active expression in evolution.

Another issue that I would like to bring into this discussion of responsibility is renunciation of responsibility. This is just as important as accepting responsibility, for it is important to know where your responsibility stops. It is important to be able to make a choice between two responsibilities or about extending your responsibility or limiting it. There are some who cannot give up a responsibility once they have taken it on; they have a belief that they are the only ones that can handle this responsibility, that it will fall apart if they leave. There is a belief that work done in a certain way or a certain pattern must go on forever that way.

So the resistances are fear of letting go of responsibility, guilt about it, fear of failing someone, belief that you are a bad person, that you will be punished if you let go of a responsibility, that there will not be support for you because you have done so. There is a lot of misunderstanding about the responsibility area. There is the area of letting others define for you what your responsibilities are, having expectations of you, and this runs into the area of perfectionism, etc., setting up impossible standards and taking on a responsibility load that you cannot handle at your present level of evolution. You may feel obliged to take on every responsibility that is asked or expected of you, feeling the responsibility of the whole world or of the whole of humanity or of the whole of the Source on your back (this leads to bad backs). You may feel guilty about enjoying yourself because you are not attending to responsibilities.

How do you know when a responsibility is finished? Well, when your soul is presenting you a new one that requires a new emphasis, a new focus. Then you can be sure that it will aid you in allowing your responsibilities to be taken on by someone else. Now, as an evolving light worker you do not just drop your responsibilities; you allow them to be assumed by another, even if you feel that the other does not work in the same way as you or cannot see the picture as well as you or does not have the savvy that you have concerning this area. Each one must always allow the newer ones to take up this new challenge for them. It is important to give them all your support, not be jealous or critical, but allow it to happen, and this will free you for your next responsibility which will also be exciting, new and challenging.

See that you can aid another in their responsibility and that brings forth another level — the level of cocreatorship. Allow yourself to share responsibility for an area, being willing to work together with other cocreators in the area of responsibility. Experience that responsibility can be shared without making a mess of it. Learn this by allowing others' input into your responsibility area and being aware of the needs of others' creativity in this area.

39

Groups – The Cocreator Level

There is only one way to achieve the true satisfaction of life, and that is to work within and acknowledge the cocreator level, or the group level, or the humanity level. As long as one tries to live as an island he or she will not bring the true energy into the cocreator level, which exists on the plane beyond the monad and connects synchronistically with the group level on the physical. The lessons are the same at all levels, it's just the energy that is different. As a matter of fact, all of you are cocreators in the infancy stage, and you just work up more and more into your cocreator group as you evolve. So what do cocreators create? Well, they create life, they create evolution just as you create your own life through your beliefs. All together you create the evolution of humanity and the Earth through your beliefs and the way you weave them together.

Now, there is a great deal of group programming, as we call it, so much indeed that it is perhaps the most heavily programmed area for all of you. For there has been a lot of betrayal, anger, jealousy, fear, pain, torture and so on connected with groups and being in a group, trying to lead a group, being a victim of a group, being surrounded by the energies of a group. Now, even if you have never belonged to a group, you can be quite sure there is some group programming there. If you can't stand to be in a room with a group very long, get panicky, then you need to look at what it is that is making you feel uncomfortable. There are many groups that have a leader, a very strong leader, and many resent the leader as an authority figure, and many of the leaders can't give up control, so there is a lot of resistance to groups.

Communication is the best way to develop a rapport with a group; and if you see a group that is having trouble, there is usually a communication problem. One needs a great deal of practice in communication and truly communicating what you feel and what you think.

Communication is the key to understanding; you can't have understanding without knowing what the other person feels, thinks or is trying to accomplish. Understanding may be looked at as standing under someone, supporting them. It allows a receptiveness to other viewpoints. If you cannot accept another's viewpoint, you can still allow yourself to accept the divinity of the one who puts forth the communication. It is the cocreator tool for evolution. There is no substitute for communication, whether you do it verbally, emotionally through your feelings, through dance, music, sound, or through a meditative state linking up with the higher qualities. It does not matter – it is all communication.

Groups, then, can be cemented and held together through

communication. The communication must keep up with the activity, must allow everyone to know what is happening and what the goals are. When there is a leader, the leader must keep in touch with all of the members of the group so that they feel included, and therefore each one is willing to give the maximum effort to further the goals; if they cannot agree on goals there will be a scattering and a differing of agendas. So the leader must be clear about the structure of the organization and about everyone's job and about the flow and how it is anticipated. The leader of a metaphysical group must be open to new experimentation, new explorations.

A metaphysical group can be of tremendous help to the Hierarchy, but it needs to be directed and yet not stifled. A good leader is necessary who will allow each one to develop to their fullest without compromising the integrity of the group or the work of the others. Sometimes this is difficult due to the programming of each member. The challenge is to be able to use the weaknesses as well as the strengths of each and weave their efforts together into one tapestry or one wholeness directed toward the goal. When there is not this working together, look then at communication and if possible at clearing. A group can be cleared as well as an individual. It is done in the same way and through the same approach.

40

Anger at the Process

Anger at the process is anger at the Source. The basic level of existence is you and your Source relationship. Certainly at this basic level you are aware of the Source's love, you have all experienced it encompassingly within that Source experience before your birth into the individualization process. Before your birth you were loved and cherished and your awareness was as comprehensive as the Source Itself. In the same way that an unborn child shares all of the resources of the structure of the mother, you shared then before being differentiated the full resources of the Source. It was a wonderful experience, one that taught you much, but the awareness was all-encompassing, not specific. Because the Source seeks to be specifically aware in all ways, It individualized Itself, brought forth unique perspectives, which is what we are, and these unique perspectives are growing and learning and evolving.

As stated over and over again in this material, your emotional perspectives are a key to the realization process. If you are holding on emotionally in a resistive way or focusing on awareness of what has been rather than what is possible now, it is very difficult to utilize the nowness opportunities. This Source-level relationship then is caught up in the emotions of what was. You remember emotionally the nurturing and the feeling of being within that Source. In the fullest sense you never left the Source, of course not, but you feel that you have because of the changing perspective, the changing environment which the Source created. When It realized It wanted a more specific process, the individualization was begun. It is important to release the feelings which keep you from recognizing that you are still as warmly supported, still as much a part of the Source as you were before entering the individualization process. An effective symbolic exercise is to re-create the feelings that you felt that were present within you before entering the individualization process and then the feelings that are present after being individualized.

Now, many of you do not recognize some of these deep emotions, and the reason is that you have buried them. In your relationship with the Creator there is some fear of your learning, of your growing. You have built in, most of you, a burying effect emotionally in order that you may consistently feel that you are making progress spiritually. If you express negative emotion or what you consider to be negative emotion, it says to many of you, "Look at that — I'm not making as much progress spiritually as I should. Here I am feeling loss or anger or resentment or frustration — I should be feeling only love and compassion and trust."

The Source set up a system through which to evolve Itself;

that system is your emotions. If you do not allow the emotion to be visible, whatever it is, you bury the key which is needed to understand why a particular experience has come to you or what you can learn from a particular experience. Yes, you can learn about it mentally, and certainly you can learn about it spiritually, but until you learn about it emotionally there will not be a physical framework in your life that reflects the clearer perspective of this learning. In other words, your emotions are the key to a physically fulfilling, rewarding and dynamically powerful life.

Going back to our Source analogy, because you fear expression of emotions if they are not positive, you begin to create a pattern of behavior which seeks to bury these emotions. Now for many of you, you had great expectations of the individualization process, and when you "sailed" through the birth canal you felt as if that expectation was not met. Thus there may be some sense of betrayal, or of bewilderment or frustration or unworthiness. "How could the Source have done anything wrong?" goes the argument; "I must have done something wrong and therefore I don't have the desired framework that I thought I would have — it's not like it was before." It is necessary to see that change through the differentiation of our Source has created, let me call it, a dynamic content in your life that was not present before.

Now, you may not consciously remember the Source before It individualized Itself. I have gone back to that point and viewed it. It is simply a less-aware state of our Sourceness. We could call it a growing up, a growth process before the Source was mature enough to assess all of Its talents and abilities and begin to recognize the dynamic content of them. Remember, on every level one must integrate a point of view before that point of view becomes available to use in a securely dynamic manner. Now, this means that when our Source reached "adulthood" — which simply means a point of realization, an integration which allowed It to recognize Its resources and begin to use them more fully — a comprehensive change occurred. You took part in this change. The Source said to all of Its aspects, "Support me in my learning and what I give you in return is your full development into the same state in which I exist."

It did not promise you that point without your step-by-step acceptance of it, though, and that's what many of you are angry about. There is also fear and loss and insecurity, but perhaps for many of you the deepest emotion is anger. The anger comes in because what you desire above all things is that comfortable, supported, beautiful alignment with the Source just as you had before. It is time to let go of It as It was, to recognize It as It is, to diffuse the anger through processing, so that your anger can become the energy resource which will allow an integration into your Source-level potential, leading eventually to the full Creator level you are seeking. It must, however, as over and over I have discussed in this material, go through the cocreator level. That is a whole other subject, discussed in several chapters of this material.

Whenever you are angry look deeply; you are angry at the process, you feel victimized by it, betrayed by it, frustrated by it, or controlled by it. There are deep emotions to release in connection with your Source relationship, and when you process these and release levels of programming, you recognize levels of energy you have not used before. This release, to be effective, must bring you then to the cocreator level.

41

Connection with the Creator and Humanity

Your connection with the Creator is, of course, basic. That Source connection is as far back as the subconscious goes, because that basic connection supports your life, your abundance, your total flow in the physical. While it sometimes mirrors as your relationship with your parent or your relationship with those-in-charge, it is always difficult if this connection is not felt clearly. If from unworthiness, or a feeling of rejection on either side or a feeling of alienation this connection is not perceived to be there, then the true clear flow of abundance and support that is available to you is not there. Now some have a very good connection with the Source, with the Creator and yet not a good connection at all with humanity, what I call the cocreator level. They cannot work with groups. Ask someone if they have trouble with groups and often they will say, "No," but ask them again, "Do you belong to any groups?" and they may say, "No, I've never joined a group" or

"I don't feel like I need to join a group, I like to do it alone. I'm a loner." There is certainly evidence there of group programming, and I would say that 75% of humanity now have some serious group programming. There is a lack of recognition by many that they are inevitably a part of a group, whether that group be the government, the Earth and all of its parts, the place where they work, the family or the many other groups formed for many other purposes.

There is no way around being a part of humanity. One is born into it, it is a part of the Creator. It is a manifestation of the Creator, and yet to much of humanity's subconscious it is in conflict with the Creator connection. There is much programming that says, "I can have either the Creator connection or the humanity or cocreator connection but not both." That says that the Creator does not want you to dilute your efforts and work with humanity or with groups. Instead, the Creator wishes you to emulate Him in his creating as a loner, so to speak, and this sounds, of course, very strange, but many who think this sounds strange have this programming. Those who must do it themselves have to be first, have to be best, cannot bear any competition, cannot bear anyone to challenge their particular expertise, can only be the leader in a group; all of this is evidence of the Creator focus that leaves out the cocreator focus. Then there are beliefs that the Creator will abandon you if you move into the cocreator level and work with groups instead of alone. And of course at the cocreator or group level there are those who feel they can only work at that level and cannot lead or be the prime creator, are not worthy, are not equal, it isn't a good idea, it isn't the way the Creator has designed life for this person. The happiest are those who recognize that both of those qualities, the ability to be creator and to be cocreator, are essential to a clear, happy and prosperous life, and that actually they are really the same thing, because the Creator in manifestation is not alone but has divided into all of Its parts, you being one of them, and so there is a group there, whether one sees it or not.

Therefore connection to both the Creator and cocreator levels is essential to fully embracing one's potential and fully enjoying life in a physical structure.

42

Will and Choice

There is some confusion on free will and choice. Many feel that if they did not have free will they would have no freedom, and freedom is greatly prized in Western society. Freedom is, to many people, an ability to make any choice they desire, to have no boundaries, to be unlimited. Their personal will makes the choice, so when they attempt to make a divine alignment, to say to the Creator, so to speak, "Thy will, not my will," or "I want to align with the Cosmic Plan and take my part in it," then it seems to the ego/personality that they are giving up free will and free choice and becoming a robot or a totally controlled being. Now, this is not really true. Surprisingly enough, even the free choices that you make outside the Divine Plan or opposed to the Divine Plan are generally stimulated by your programming, and so actually free will choices are mainly your programming taking you to various areas that are detours from your true part in the Plan. Now, the

Divine Plan has your part in it as a clear and most direct way to proceed with your evolution and also to aid humanity, the Earth, etc. As long as you avoid using that Plan and take a detour, then you are holding up all of these things, but the Creator doesn't mind. The Creator is very allowing and you may take as many detours as you like, you may hold up as much as you like, the system can absorb it and it does. However, your own peace of mind, your own joy, your own happiness follow from surrendering to the Plan and thereby moving in a rather direct path to the next step in your evolution through whatever service to humanity and yourself is selected for you from your past experience.

Now, when I say you surrender to the Plan, that doesn't mean that you are totally controlled, not at all; you have various broad objectives which you pursue then in your own way, in a way that your experience and education and knowledge and position allow because when you ask for the soul guidance through surrendering, the soul then takes over and moves you into this wider Plan that it has, its purpose for coming to Earth, and it knows how to do it very well, and so there is a feeling of accomplishment, of achievement, of using the dynamic energy more fully and the receptive energy more completely and blending them well as you move forward in your evolution. It doesn't mean that your path will necessarily be easy but it will not seem difficult. You will do many very important and valuable services without stress, without anger, without resistance, and that indeed is the goal for many in physical existence.

So look at why, if you cannot surrender to the Cosmic Plan, to the Divine Plan. Is there a belief that it is flawed?, that it will take advantage of you and use you, that you will lose your own identity? Does your ego/personality fight it and feel that it will be wiped out? Work on those areas of programming until you can allow yourself to feel that surrender to the larger needs of your evolution, where you can see beyond your own needs and yet include your own needs.

HOT OFF THE PRESSES AT . . .
LIGHT TECHNOLOGY PUBLISHING

THE ASCENSION BOOK SERIES by Joshua David Stone

THE COMPLETE ASCENSION MANUAL: How to Achieve Ascension in This Lifetime
BOOK I   A synthesis of the past and guidance for ascension. This book is an extraordinary compendium of practical techniques and spiritual history. Compiled from research and channeled information, it offers specific steps to accelerate our process of ascension — here and now!

ISBN 0-929385-55-1 $14.95

SOUL PSYCHOLOGY: Keys To Ascension
BOOK II   Modern psychology deals exclusively with personality, ignoring the dimensions of spirit and soul. This book provides ground-breaking theories and techniques for healing and self-realization.

ISBN 0-929385-56-X $14.95

BEYOND ASCENSION: How to Complete the Seven Levels of Initiation
BOOK III   This book brings forth incredible new channeled material that completely demystifies the seven levels of initiation and how to attain them. It contains revolutionary new information on how to anchor and open our 36 chakras and how to build our light quotient at a rate of speed never dreamed possible.

ISBN 0-929385-73-X $14.95

HIDDEN MYSTERIES: An Overview of History's Secrets from Mystery Schools to ET Contacts   BOOK IV   An exploration of the unknown and suppressed aspects of our planet's past, it reveals new information on the extraterrestrial movement and secret teachings of the ancient Master schools, Egyptians and Essenes.

ISBN 0-929385-57-8 $14.95

THE ASCENDED MASTERS LIGHT THE WAY: Keys to Spiritual Mastery from Those Who Achieved It   BOOK V   The lives and teachings of forty of the world's greatest Saints and spiritual beacons provide a blueprint for total self-realization. Inspiring guidance from those who learned the secrets of mastery in their lifetimes.

ISBN 0-929385-58-6 $14.95

ASCENSION ACTIVATION TAPES:
How to anchor and open your 36 chakras and build your light quotient at a speed never dreamed possible. Hundreds of new ascension techniques and meditations directly from the galactic and universal core.

ASCENSION ACTIVATION MEDITATION TAPE	S101	$12.00
TREE OF LIFE ASCENSION MEDITATION TAPE	S102	$12.00
MT. SHASTA ASCENSION ACTIVATION MEDITATIONS	S103	$12.00
KABBALISTIC ASCENSION ACTIVATION	S104	$12.00
COMPLETE ASCENSION MANUAL MEDITATION	S105	$12.00
SET OF ALL 5 TAPES	S110	$49.95

ARRIVING SOON from our presses . . .

POISONS THAT HEAL by Eileen Nauman, DHM, DIHom (UK)
Homeopathy to Survive the Deadly Epidemics

Modern medicine has failed us! Antibiotics are failing us. Vaccinations have already failed us. What's left between us and the deadly super bugs and viruses that are already stalking and killing us? Homeopathic medicine.
Learn how to protect yourself and your family against the Ebola Virus, the Hanta Virus, Whooping Cough epidemics, Lyme Disease and flesh-eating Strep A. This book also offers:

✦ Homeopathic remedies for menopause — there is an alternative to cancer-causing Hormone Replacement Therapy (HRT).
✦ First-aid and acute homeopathic remedies for everyday ailments such as colds, flu, measles and more . . .
✦ Vital information on how to contact a homeopath, a homeopathic study group, and homeopathic pharmacies for medicine kits, as well as where to receive training.
✦ A Materia Medica with homeopathic remedies for the epidemics and concise symptom pictures.

ISBN 0-929385-62-4 $14.95

EVOLUTION — OUR LOOP OF EXPERIENCING by Vywamus, Djwhal Khul and Atlanto, channeled by Janet McClure. Sample chapters are:

✦ Your Four Bodies
✦ Casting Off the Chrysalis
✦ Evolution — Our Loop of Experiencing
✦ The Input of Higher Consciousness
✦ Restructuring the Cellular Level
✦ The Tibetan Lesson Series
✦ Other Dimensions
✦ Time and Space
✦ The Cosmic Walk-In
✦ The Twelve Rays

ISBN 0-929385-54-3 $14.95

BOOK MARKET

A reader's guide to the extraordinary books we publish, print and market for your enLightenment.

BOOKS BY DOROTHY ROEDER

THE NEXT DIMENSION IS LOVE
Ranoash through **Dorothy Roeder**
As speaker for a civilization whose species is more advanced, the entity describes the help they offer humanity by clearing the DNA. An exciting vision of our possibilities and future.

$11.95 Softcover 148 pp.　ISBN 0-929385-50-0

REACH FOR US Your Cosmic Teachers and Friends
Channeled by **Dorothy Roeder**
Messages from Teachers, Ascended Masters and the Space Command explain the role they play in bringing the Divine Plan to the earth now!

$13.00 Softcover 168 pp.　ISBN 0-929385-69-1

CRYSTAL CO-CREATORS
Channeled by **Dorothy Roeder**
A fascinating exploration of 100 forms of crystals, describing specific uses and their purpose, from the spiritual to the cellular, as agents of change. It clarifies the role of crystals in our awakening.

$14.95 Softcover　ISBN 0-929385-40-3

SHINING THE LIGHT BOOK II
by **Light Technology Research**
Continuing the story of the Secret Government and alien involvement. Also information about the Photon Belt, cosmic holograms photographed in the sky, a new vortex forming near Sedona, and nefarious mining on sacred Hopi land.

$14.95 Softcover　ISBN 0-929385-70-5

LIVING RAINBOWS
by **Gabriel H. Bain**
A fascinating "how-to" manual to make experiencing human, astral, animal and plant auras an everyday event. Series of techniques, exercises and illustrations guide the simply curious to see and hear aural energy. Spiral-bound workbook format.

$14.95 Softcover　ISBN 0-929385-42-X

POISONS THAT HEAL
by Dr. Eileen Nauman DHM (U.K.)
Homeopathy is all that remains to protect us from the deadly super bugs and viruses that modern medicine has failed to turn back. Learn how to protect yourself and your family against the coming Ebola virus and other deadly diseases. Valuable remedies for menopause, first aid and everyday ailments. Homeopathic resources and Materia medica.

$14.95 Softcover 270 pages　ISBN 0-929385-62-4

COLOR MEDICINE The Secrets of Color Vibrational Healing
by **Charles Klotsche**
A practitioners' manual for restoring blocked energy to the body systems and organs with specific color wavelengths by the founder of "The 49th Vibrational Technique."

$11.95 Softcover 114 pp.　ISBN 0-929385-27-6

TEMPLE OF THE LIVING EARTH
by Nicole Christine
An intimate true story that activates the realization that the Living Earth is our Temple and that we are all Priests and Priestesses to the World. A call to the human spirit to celebrate life and awaken to its cocreative partnership with Earth. Nicole Chistine invites you into the inner chambers of her consciousness and charts a pathway to your authentic Self.

$16.00 Softcover 160 pages　ISBN 0-9647306-0-X

BEHOLD A PALE HORSE
by **Bill Cooper**
Former U.S. Naval Intelligence Briefing Team Member reveals information kept secret by our government since the 1940s. UFOs, assassination, the Secret Government, the war on drugs and more by the world's leading expert on UFOs.

$25.00 Softcover 500 pp.　ISBN 0-929385-22-5

THE SEDONA VORTEX GUIDEBOOK
by **12 various channels**
200-plus pages of channeled, never-before published information on the vortex energies of Sedona and the techniques to enable you to use the vortexes as multidimensional portals to time, space and other realities.

$14.95 Softcover 236 pp.　ISBN 0-929385-25-X

COMING SOON!
THE EXPLORER RACE A channeled book
by **Robert Shapiro**
In this expansive overview, Zoosh explains, "You are the Explorer Race. Learn about your journey before coming to this Earth, your evolution here and what lies ahead." Topics range from ETs and UFOs to relationships.

$24.95 Softcover 650 pp.　ISBN 0-929385-38-1

SHINING THE LIGHT
by **Light Technology Research**
Revelations about the Secret Government and their connections with ETs. Information about renegade ETs mining the Moon, ancient Pleiadian warships, underground alien bases and many more startling facts.

$12.95 Softcover　ISBN 0-929385-66-7

BOOK MARKET

BOOK MARKET

BOOK MARKET

BOOKS BY TOM DONGO

NEW! MERGING DIMENSIONS
by Tom Dongo and Linda Bradshaw

Photographs of strange events, other woldly beings, strange flying craft. unexplained light anamolies - THEY'RE LEAVING PHYSICAL EVIDENCE!

$14.95 Softcover 160pp.   ISBN 0-9622748-4-4

UNSEEN BEINGS UNSEEN WORLDS
by Tom Dongo

Venture into unknown realms with a leading researcher. Discover new information on how to communicate with nonphysical beings, aliens, ghosts, wee people and the Gray zone. Photos of ET activity and interaction with humans.

$9.95 Softcover 122 pp.   ISBN 0-9622748-3-6

**THE QUEST
The Mysteries of Sedona III**
by Tom Dongo

Fascinating in-depth interviews with 26 who have answered the call to Sedona and speak of their spiritual experiences. Explores the mystique of the area and effect the quests have had on individual lives.

Photos/illustrations.

$8.95 Softcover 144 pp.   ISBN 0-9622748-2-8

**THE ALIEN TIDE
The Mysteries of Sedona II**
by Tom Dongo

The UFO and ET events and para-normal activity in the Sedona area and nationwide are investigated and detailed by a leading researcher who cautions against fear of the alien presence. Intriguing information for all who seek new insights. Photos/illustrations.

$7.95 Softcover 128 pp.   ISBN 0-9622748-1-X

THE MYSTERIES OF SEDONA
THE NEW AGE FRONTIER
by Tom Dongo

An overview of the New Age Mecca that is Sedona, Arizona. Topics are the famous energy vortexes, UFOs, channeling, Lemuria, metaphysical and mystical experiences and area paranormal activity. Photos/illustrations.

$6.95 Softcover 84 pp.   ISBN 0-96227480-0-1

**OUT-OF-BODY EXPLORATION
A Guide to New Dimensions of Self-realization**
by Jerry Mulvin

Techniques for traveling in the Soul Body to achieve absolute freedom and experience truth for oneself,. Discover reincarnation, karma and your personal spiritual path.

$8.95 Softcover   ISBN 0-941464-01-6

BOOKS BY RICHARD DANNELLEY

SEDONA POWER SPOT, Vortex and Medicine Wheel Guide
by Richard Dannelley

Dicover why this book is so popular! Six detailed maps, special meditations for each power spot, and a lot of heart - Richard Dannelley is a native of the Sedona area.

$11.00 Softcover   ISBN 0-9629453-2-3

**NEW! SEDONA: BEYOND THE VORTEX
The Ultimate Journey to Your Personal Place of Power**
by Richard Dannelley

An advanced guide to ascension, using vortex power, sacred geometry, and the Merkaba.

$12.00 Softcover   ISBN 0-9629453-4-3

BOOKS BY LYNN BUESS

NUMEROLOGY FOR THE NEW AGE
by Lynn Buess M.A., Ed.S.

An established standard, explicating for contemporary readers the ancient art and science of symbol, cycle, and vibration. Provides insights into the patterns of our personal lives.
Includes life and Personality Numbers.

$9.85 Softcover 262 pp.   ISBN 0-929385-31-4

BOOKS BY RUTH RYDEN

THE GOLDEN PATH
Channeled by Ruth Ryden

"Book of Lessons" by the master teachers explaining the process of channeling. Akashic Records, karma, opening the third eye, the ego and the meaning of Bible stories. It is a master class for opening your personal pathway.

$11.95 Softcover 200 pp.   ISBN 0-929385-43-8

**LIVING THE GOLDEN PATH
Practical Soul-utions to Today's Problems**
Channeled by Ruth Ryden

Guidance that can be used in the real world to solve dilemmas — to strengthen inner resolves and see the Light at the end of the road. Covers the difficult issues of failure, addictions, drugs, personal tragedies, rape, abortion, and suicide.

$11.95 Softcover 186 pp.   ISBN 0-929385-65-9

NUMEROLOGY: NUANCES IN RELATIONSHIPS
by Lynn Buess M.A., Ed.S.

Provides valuable assistance in the quest to better understand compatibilities and conflicts with a significant other. A handy guide for calculating your/his/her personality numbers.

$12.65 Softcover 239 pp.   ISBN 0-929385-23-3

BOOKS BY WES BATEMAN

KNOWLEDGE FROM THE STARS
by Wes Bateman

A telepath with contact to ETs, Bateman has provided a wide spectrum of scientific information. A fascinating compilation of articles surveying the Federation, ETs, evolution and the trading houses, all part of the true history of the galaxy.

$11.95 Softcover 171 pp.   ISBN 0-929385-39-X

DRAGONS AND CHARIOTS
by Wes Bateman

An explanation of spacecraft, propulsion systems, gravity, the Dragon, manipulated Light and inter-stellar and intergalactic motherships by a renowned telepath who details specific technological information he has been given through contact with ETs.

$9.95 Softcover 65 pp.   ISBN 0-929385-45-4

CHILDREN OF LIGHT: CHILDREN OF DENIAL
by Lynn Buess M.A., Ed.S.

In his fourth book Lynn calls upon his decades of practice as counselor and psychotherapist to explore the relationship between karma and the new insights from ACOA/ Co-dependency writings.

$8.95 Softcover 150 pp.   ISBN 0-929385-15-2

BOOK MARKET

B O O K   M A R K E T   O R D E R   F O R M

BOOKS PUBLISHED BY LIGHT TECHNOLOGY PUBLISHING

		NO. COPIES	TOTAL			NO. COPIES	TOTAL
ACUPRESSURE FOR THE SOUL *Fallon*	$11.95	___	$ _____	**Arthur Fanning**			
				SOULS, EVOLUTION & the FATHER	$12.95	___	$ _____
ALIEN PRESENCE *Ananda*	$19.95	___	$ _____	SIMON	$9.95	___	$ _____
BEHOLD A PALE HORSE *Cooper*	$25.00	___	$ _____	**Wesley H. Bateman**			
				DRAGONS AND CHARIOTS	$9.95	___	$ _____
CHANNELLING *Vywamus/Burns*	$9.95	___	$ _____	KNOWLEDGE FROM THE STARS	$11.95	___	$ _____
COLOR MEDICINE *Klotsche*	$11.95	___	$ _____	**Lynn Buess**			
				CHILDREN OF LIGHT . . .	$8.95	___	$ _____
EXPLORER RACE *Shapiro*	$24.95	___	$ _____	NUMEROLOGY: Nuances	$12.65	___	$ _____
				NUMEROLOGY for the NEW AGE	$9.85	___	$ _____
FOREVER YOUNG *Clark*	$9.95	___	$ _____	**Hallie Deering**			
				LIGHT FROM THE ANGELS	$15.00	___	$ _____
LEGEND OF THE EAGLE CLAN *Cramer*	$12.95	___	$ _____	DO-IT-YOURSELF POWER TOOLS	$25.00	___	$ _____
LIVING RAINBOWS *Bain*	$14.95	___	$ _____	**Dorothy Roeder**			
				CRYSTAL CO-CREATORS	$14.95	___	$ _____
MAHATMA I & II *Grattan*	$19.95	___	$ _____	NEXT DIMENSION IS LOVE	$11.95	___	$ _____
				REACH FOR US	$13.00	___	$ _____
NEW AGE PRIMER	$11.95	___	$ _____	**Ruth Ryden**			
POISONS THAT HEAL *Nauman*	$14.95	___	$ _____	THE GOLDEN PATH	$11.95	___	$ _____
				LIVING THE GOLDEN PATH	$11.95	___	$ _____
PRISONERS OF EARTH *Starr*	$11.95	___	$ _____	**Joshua David Stone, Ph.D.**			
				COMPLETE ASCENSION MANUAL	$14.95	___	$ _____
SHINING THE LIGHT	$12.95	___	$ _____	SOUL PSYCHOLOGY	$14.95	___	$ _____
SHINING THE LIGHT — BOOK II	$14.95	___	$ _____	BEYOND ASCENSION	$14.95	___	$ _____
SEDONA VORTEX GUIDE BOOK	$14.95	___	$ _____	HIDDEN MYSTERIES	$14.95	___	$ _____
SHADOW OF S.F. PEAKS *Bader*	$9.95	___	$ _____	ASCENDED MASTERS	$14.95	___	$ _____
				Vywamus/Janet McClure			
STORY OF THE PEOPLE *Rota*	$11.95	___	$ _____	AHA! THE REALIZATION BOOK	$11.95	___	$ _____
				LIGHT TECHNIQUES	$11.95	___	$ _____
THIS WORLD AND NEXT ONE *"Aiello"*	$9.95	___	$ _____	SANAT KUMARA	$11.95	___	$ _____
				SCOPES OF DIMENSIONS	$11.95	___	$ _____
				THE SOURCE ADVENTURE	$11.95	___	$ _____
				EVOLUTION: LOOP OF EXPERIENCING	$14.95	___	$ _____

BOOKS PRINTED OR MARKETED BY LIGHT TECHNOLOGY PUBLISHING

		NO. COPIES	TOTAL			NO. COPIES	TOTAL
ASCENSION HANDBOOK *Stubbs*	$11.95	___	$ _____	SPIRIT OF THE NINJA *Siege*	$7.95	___	$ _____
AWAKEN TO THE HEALER WITHIN *Work, Groth*	$14.95	___	$ _____	TALKS WITH JONATHON *Miller*	$14.95	___	$ _____
DEDICATED TO THE SOUL . . . *Vosacek*	$9.95	___	$ _____	**Richard Dannelley**			
E.T. 101 INSTR. MANUAL *Mission Control*	$12.00	___	$ _____	SEDONA POWER SPOT/GUIDE	$11.00	___	$ _____
EXPLORING LIFE'S LAST FRONTIER *Harder*	$15.95	___	$ _____	SEDONA: BEYOND THE VORTEX	$12.00	___	$
"I'M OK . . ." *Golden Star Alliance*	$6.00	___	$ _____	**Tom Dongo: Mysteries of Sedona**			
INANNA RETURNS *Ferguson*	$14.00	___	$ _____	MYSTERIES OF SEDONA—Book I	$6.95	___	$ _____
IT'S TIME TO REMEMBER *Gilbert*	$19.95	___	$ _____	ALIEN TIDE—Book II	$7.95	___	$ _____
I WANT TO KNOW *Starr*	$7.00	___	$ _____	QUEST—Book III	$8.95	___	$ _____
GREAT KACHINA *Bader*	$9.95	___	$ _____	UNSEEN BEINGS . . .	$9.95	___	$ _____
LIFE ON THE CUTTING EDGE *Rachelle*	$14.95	___	$ _____	MERGING DIMENSIONS	$14.95	___	$ _____
OUR COSMIC ANCESTORS *Chatelain*	$9.95	___	$ _____	**Preston B. Nichols with Peter Moon**			
OUT OF BODY EXPLORATION *Mulvin*	$8.95	___	$ _____	MONTAUK PROJECT	$15.95	___	$ _____
PRINCIPLES TO REMEMBER *Maile*	$11.95	___	$ _____	MONTAUK REVISITED	$19.95	___	$ _____
SONG OF SIRIUS *McManus*	$8.00	___	$ _____	PYRAMIDS OF MONTAUK	$19.95	___	$ _____
SOUL RECOVERY/EXTRACTION *Waya*	$9.95	___	$ _____	**Lyssa Royal and Keith Priest**			
TEMPLE OF THE LIVING EARTH *Christine*	$14.95	___	$ _____	PREPARING FOR CONTACT	$12.95	___	$ _____
THE ONLY PLANET OF CHOICE *Schlemmer*	$14.95	___	$ _____	PRISM OF LYRA	$11.95	___	$ _____
TOUCHED BY LOVE *McManus*	$9.95	___	$ _____	VISITORS FROM WITHIN	$12.95	___	$ _____
WE ARE ONE *Norquist*	$14.95	___	$ _____				

ASCENSION MEDITATION TAPES

		NO. COPIES	TOTAL			NO. COPIES	TOTAL
Joshua David Stone, Ph.D.				**Brian Grattan**			
Ascension Activation Meditation	$12.00	___	$ _____	Seattle Seminar Resurrection 1994 (12 tapes)	$79.95	___	$ _____
Tree of Life Ascension Meditation	$12.00	___	$ _____	**YHWH/Arthur Fanning**			
Mt. Shasta Ascension Activation Meditation	$12.00	___	$ _____	On Becoming	$10.00	___	$ _____
Kabbalistic Ascension Activation	$12.00	___	$ _____	Healing Meditations/Knowing Self	$10.00	___	$ _____
Complete Ascension Manual Meditation	$12.00	___	$ _____	Manifestation & Alignment w/ Poles	$10.00	___	$ _____
Set of all 5 tapes	$49.95	___	$ _____	The Art of Shutting Up	$10.00	___	$ _____
Vywamus/Barbara Burns				Continuity of Consciousness	$25.00	___	$ _____
The Quantum Mechanical You (6 tapes)	$40.00	___	$ _____	Black Hole Meditation	$10.00	___	$ _____
				Merging the Golden Light Replicas of You	$10.00	___	$ _____

BOOKSTORE DISCOUNTS HONORED

SEND ☐ CHECK OR ☐ MONEY ORDER
(U.S. FUNDS ONLY) PAYABLE TO:
LIGHT TECHNOLOGY PUBLISHING
P.O. BOX 1526 • SEDONA • AZ 86339
(520) 282-6523   FAX: (520) 282-4130
1-800-450-0985

NAME/COMPANY _____

ADDRESS _____

CITY/STATE/ZIP _____

PHONE _____ CONTACT _____

All prices in US$. Higher in Canada and Europe.

SUBTOTAL: $ _____
SALES TAX: $ _____
(7.5% – AZ residents only)
SHIPPING/HANDLING: $ _____
(*3 Min.; 10% of orders over *30)
CANADA S/H: $ _____
(20% of order)
TOTAL AMOUNT ENCLOSED: $ _____

CANADA: CHEROV CANADA, INC. 1(800) 263-2408 FAX (519) 986-3103 • ENGLAND/EUROPE: WINDRUSH PRESS LTD. 0608 652012/652025 FAX 0608 652125
AUSTRALIA: GEMCRAFT BOOKS (03)888-0111 FAX (03)888-0044 • SPECTRUM ACCESS (617)357-1555 FAX (617)357-1771 • NEW ZEALAND: PEACEFUL LIVING PUB. (07)571-8105 FAX (07)571-8513